Journey Through the Great Fast

Published by

**Office of Religious Education
Archeparchy of Pittsburgh**

November 2001

DEDICATION

This edition of Journey Through the Great Fast is dedicated to the memory of ✝Metropolitan Judson M. Procyk, who passed from this life as we worked on this project. The people who serve in the many programs of the Office of Religious Education will sadly miss his inspiration, encouragement and support.

Vičnaja jemu pamjat'!
Eternal Memory!

Published by
The Office of Religious Education
Archeparchy of Pittsburgh
3605 Perrysville Avenue
Pittsburgh, PA 15214

Steve Puluka, Managing Editor
Kathryn Siglow Kress, Editor
Jack Figel, Design and Layout

Contributors
Clergy and Laity of the
Byzantine Catholic Metropolia of Pittsburgh

Cover Icons
Judy Lauderbaugh, Front
Solrunn Nes, Back

Liturgical texts from the *Lenten Triodion*,
Sisters of Saint Basil, Uniontown, PA

Scripture references from the *Typicon* by Father David Petras, SEOD

Produced by
Eastern Christian Publications, PO Box 146, Fairfax, VA 22030

ISBN: 1-892278-16-2

TABLE OF CONTENTS

PREFACE

The liturgical year of our church presents us with two cycles of feasts that we celebrate. The *fixed feasts* that we celebrate, those like the Nativity and Theophany of Christ, are celebrated on the same date each year. These feasts tell us about the content of our faith, <u>what</u> we believe about the Incarnation, the Holy Trinity, about our Transfiguration into godlike people. The *moveable feasts,* such as the Resurrection, the Ascension and Pentecost fall on different dates each year based on the Spring equinox. These moveable feasts tell us <u>how</u> we can become godlike people. Our preparation for Pascha gives us direction.

During the Great Fast journey we are presented with the themes of repentance and renewal, asceticism and fasting, conversion and change of heart. We are asked to take on a *Lenten style of life*.

This book can serve as a map for our Great Fast journey. It contains reflections of men and women in our church who strive to become godlike people. They invite you to listen as the liturgical texts speak about a *springtime of renewal*. These prayers, hymns and meditations provide us with insights and suggestions for making this time a rich season in our lives.

At the Office of Religious Education for the Archeparchy of Pittsburgh, our hope and prayer is that the *Journey Through the Great Fast* guides you into the marvelous light of the Resurrection.

S' nami Boh! God is with us!

Sister Marion Dobos, OSB
Director, Office of Religious Education

Father Elias L. Rafaj
Assistant Director, Office of Religious Education

Editor's Note: I would like to thank each and every contributor to this project. If in the writing, you found a blessing, I can assure you that I was blessed many times over while editing your articles. The richness of our Eastern spirituality poured out in abundance on every page as you called us to repentance and fasting. This book will prove a feast of manna in the desert of the Great Fast. God grant you many blessed years!

SUNDAY OF ZACCHEUS

Father Joseph Kapusnak

As salvation came to the house of Zaccheus by Your entrance, O Christ; likewise now by the entrance of your sacred ministers, and Your holy angels with them, grant peace to this house and mercifully bless it, saving and enlightening all who live within.

Troparion

Readings

1 Timothy 4:9-15

Luke 19:1-10

Meditation

Lord, your mercy is great indeed for all who receive it with sincerity of heart. And we rejoice today with Zaccheus, the poor little rich man whose house was blessed and sanctified by your entrance and Presence.

Listening to this holy gospel, we understand that even though he had a certain amount of material wealth and earthly riches, he himself realized that there was something missing and that indeed, he was poor.

But he could only have known this because he responded to your invitation, gently but insistently, calling to his heart. His heart must have been a heart of flesh, warm and giving (and also unusual for a tax collector – a chief tax collector, at that!), for he says that he gives "one half of his possessions to the poor" and will "restore fourfold if he has defrauded anyone."

No, this Zaccheus is not a cold and calculating man, but a man in search of that "something missing" in his life. Even though he did not know what it was, he did know in his heart that somehow this Jesus might have the answer for him.

Jesus, your answer came, in a manner that by far exceeded his expectations and imaginings. For he came to realize in the instant that You said, "Zaccheus, come down immediately..." that You, O Lord, were the only "true riches". And how he rejoiced when You invited him, to invite You to his house.

O noble Zaccheus, your immediate response shows us your heart: a heart now fully enlightened by the "Enlightener of Hearts". Your heart is ready to know and do the will of He who came, not only to stay in your home, but to make his home in your heart and your life. And so we too, rejoice with you today.

Icon of Christ and Zaccheus

Lord, as the time of the Great Fast so swiftly approaches, give to me the desire of Zaccheus to see You: the desire that will go any lengths and do anything to get just a glimpse of You. For I know, O Lord, that it is far more than just a "glimpse" that You give to those who "seek You with all their heart."

It is You, One God, Father, Son, and Holy Spirit that You desire to give to us ... to me. "Create a pure heart in me, O Lord."

Patristic Reading

"Salvation comes to the house" of Zaccheus even. For what reason? Was it because he also believed that Christ came by Marcion? But the blind man's cry was still sounding in the ears of all: "Jesus, Son of David, have mercy on me." And "all the people gave praise unto God"– not Marcion's, but David's.

Now, although Zaccheus was probably a Gentile, he yet from his intercourse with Jews had obtained a smattering of their Scriptures, and, more than this, had, without knowing it, fulfilled the precepts of Isaiah: "Deal thy bread," said the prophet, "to the hungry, and bring the poor that are cast out into thine house." This he did in the best possible way, by receiving the Lord, and entertaining Him in his house.

"When thou seest the naked, cover him." This he promised to do, in an equally satisfactory way, when he offered the half of his goods for all works of mercy. So also "he loosened the bands of wickedness, undid the heavy burdens, let the oppressed go free, and broke every yoke," when he said, "If I have taken anything from any man by false accusation, I restore him fourfold." Therefore the Lord said, "This day is salvation come to this house."

Thus did He give his testimony, that the precepts of the Creator spoken by the prophet tended to salvation. But when He adds, "or the Son of man is come to seek and to save that which is lost," my present contention is not whether He was come to save what was lost, to whom it had once belonged, and from whom what He came to save had fallen away; but I approach a different question. Man, there can be no doubt of it, is here the subject of consideration.

Now, since he consists of two parts, body and soul, the point to be inquired into is, in which of these two, man would seem to have been lost? If in his body, then it is his body, not his soul, which is lost. What, whoever is lost, the Son of man saves. The body, therefore, has the salvation. If, on the other hand, it is in his soul that man is lost, salvation is designed for the lost soul; and the body which is not lost is safe.

If, to take the only the only other supposition, man is wholly lost, in both his natures, then it necessarily follows that salvation is appointed for the entire man; and then the opinion of the heretics is shivered to pieces, who say that there is no salvation of the flesh. And this affords a confirmation that Christ belongs to the Creator, who followed the Creator in promising the salvation of the whole man.

Tertullian, Against Marcion

Reflection Questions

- Put yourself in the Gospel scene. Who am I? Zaccheus? One of the people who want to see Jesus? Who murmured against Jesus? Who wants to harm Jesus?

- Why?

SUNDAY OF THE PUBLICAN AND PHARISEE

Lector Jack Figel, Deacon Candidate

O faithful, let us repeat the words of the Publican who said in the Temple: "O God be merciful to me," so that together with him we may receive forgiveness of our sins without falling into the error of the boastful Pharisee.

Matins Canon, Ode 8

Readings

2 Timothy 3:10-15

Luke 18:10-14

Meditation

A little while ago, there were two Byzantine Catholic priests and a deacon in our rectory office discussing the most appropriate position for prayer. The first priest said that he felt standing with his arms at his side and with his eyes closed was the most appropriate position. The second said that clasping his hands together on his chest was the best. The deacon said that making a complete prostration, laying flat on the floor, was the most powerful position for prayer.

There was also a telephone repairman in the office working on a new phone line for the parish computer. He overhead this conversation and added: "well, I made the most powerful prayer of my life when I was hanging upside down by my heels from a telephone pole forty feet in the air!"

So what position do we take when WE pray? In today's Gospel reading, we see two positions. The Pharisee was praying with himself, standing tall and erect, proud of his supposed religious life. The Gospel does not tell us exactly where the Pharisee stood, but says "his normal place." I can just imagine he was up front where all could see him clearly. Meanwhile, the Publican, or tax collector, took a position of humility. He stood in the back of the Temple, his eyes lowered and head bowed, beating his breast and asking forgiveness from God.

Which of these two positions were truly repentant? Which of these were truly honest in their prayer?

As we prepare to begin the Great Fast in a few weeks, are we in the right "spiritual position" for prayer? Are we honest with God in our prayer? Do we have the right state of mind as we ask God to forgive our sins?

Icon of the Publican and Pharisee

There is a prayer that we all know by heart and say very often—the Our Father. It has a phrase that forces us to be honest with God and be in the right spiritual position for prayer. "Forgive us our trespasses, as we forgive those who trespass against us." In this prayer, we ask God to forgive our sins, as we forgive others. However, if we have NOT forgiven others, will God forgive us? I don't think so!

Have we truly forgiven others who have wronged us?

For example, in our family – if one of the kids used the phone too long on the internet and we couldn't make a phone call, or if our spouse yelled at us for being late getting ready for church, have we forgiven them?

With our neighbors – if the kids down the street trampled the flower beds with their bikes, or if our friends at school didn't let us join in the basketball game at lunchtime, have we forgiven them?

With people we meet in the shopping mall – if someone cuts in front of us in the checkout line, or if some other kid is playing our favorite video game when we want to, have we forgiven them?

Before we can ask God to forgive our own sins, we must forgive all others – ALL others, not just those who we like! God does not discriminate and neither can we!

We are about to share in the Great Fast, a pilgrimage toward Good Friday and ultimately Resurrection on Holy Pascha. Let us all get into the right "spiritual position" by being honest with God in our prayer. Let us turn into action the words of the prayer of Saint Ephrem that we use throughout the Lenten period: "grant me the grace to be aware of my sins and not to judge others."

Patristic Reading

The Christian ought not to grudge another's reputation, nor rejoice over any man's faults; he ought in Christ's love to grieve and be afflicted at his brother's faults, and rejoice over his brother's good deeds. He ought not to be indifferent or silent before sinners. He who shows another to be wrong ought to do so with all tenderness, in the fear of God, and with the object of converting the sinner. He who is proved wrong or rebuked ought to take it willingly, recognizing his own gain in being set right. When any one is being accused, it is not right for another, before him or any one else, to contradict the accuser; but if at any time the charge seems groundless to any one, he ought privately to enter into discussion with the accuser, and either produce, or acquire, conviction.

Every one ought, as far as he is able, to conciliate one who has ground of complaint against him. No one ought to cherish a grudge against the sinner who repents, but heartily to forgive him. He who says that he has repented of a sin ought not only to be pricked with compunction for his sin, but also to bring forth fruits worthy of repentance. He who has been corrected in first faults, and received pardon, if he sins again, prepares for himself a judgment of wrath worse than the former. He, who after the first and second admonition abides in his fault, ought to be brought before the person in authority, if haply after being rebuked by more he may be ashamed.

If even thus he fail to be set right, he is to be cut off from the rest as one that maketh to offend, and regarded as a heathen and a publican, for the security of them that are obedient, according to the saying: when the impious fall, the righteous tremble.

Basil, Letter XXII

Reflection Questions

- Do we truly live the phrase from the Lord's Prayer: "forgive us our trespasses as we forgive those who trespass against us"?

- Each evening as we go to sleep, have we forgiven those who have wronged us during that day?

- Are we more like the Pharisee and proud of our piety, or more like the Publican and constantly ask God for forgiveness of our sins?

SUNDAY OF THE PRODIGAL SON

Monk Elias, O. Carm.

Hasten to open your fatherly arms, O Lord, for I have foolishly wasted my whole life. In the inexhaustible treasury of your mercy, O Savior, do not despise the poverty of my heart. I cry to You, O Lord, full of compunction: Father, I have sinned against heaven and against you.

Matins Sessional Hymn, Tone 1

Readings

1 Corinthians 6:12-20

Luke 15:11-32

Meditation

It is me, O Lord. I am the Prodigal.

O Lord, Jesus Christ, your story pierces my heart, for you have perfectly described my own experience of life. Your Word is truly a sword that knows its mark, and it has found its place. It is me, O Lord. I am the Prodigal. I have wasted so much of my time, so many of your gifts. I have squandered your riches unworthily.

But I take such comfort, that this story is not only about me. Before me, in your Word, I see the Father. Rather, the Father sees me from "afar off". He is there waiting for my return, hoping for my repentance, lovingly anticipating a wonderful reconciliation. If I have disappointed Him by my foolish choices in the past, I will not disappoint Him today. I will return to my Father and my God. I will return to his embrace and ask forgiveness. I will repent.

I remember a story from the life of Abba Moses:

A brother asked the old man, "Here is a man who beats his servant because of a fault he has committed; what will the servant say?" The old man said, "If the servant is good, he should say, 'Forgive me, for I have sinned'." The brother said to him, "Nothing else"? The old man said, "No, for from the moment he takes upon himself the responsibility for the affair and says, 'I have sinned,' immediately his master will have mercy on him."

It is me, O Lord. I am the Prodigal. Grant me also a true spirit of repentance. Make me your true servant who accepts responsibility for my failings, and grant me the courage to face you and say, "Forgive me, for I have sinned." Today, let me know your love; let me experience your holy embrace. Set the feast and prepare the banquet table. Grant that by my reception today of your Holy Mysteries, my repentance will be made perfect, and our reconciliation complete.

Icon of the Story of the Prodigal Son

Patristic Reading

Now he who has been counted worthy of the heavenly calling, and by this calling has been sanctified, if he grow negligent in it although washed becomes defiled: "counting the blood of the covenant by which he was sanctified a profane thing, and despising the Spirit of grace," he hears the words, "Friend, how camest thou in hither, not having wedding garments?" For the banquet of the saints is spotless and pure: "for many are called, but few chosen." Judas to wit, though he came to the supper, because he despised it went out from the presence of the Lord, and having abandoned his life, hanged himself. But the disciples who continued with the Redeemer shared in the happiness of the feast.

And that young man who went into a far country, and there wasted his substance, living in dissipation, if he receive a desire for this divine feast, and coming to himself, shall say, "How many hired servants of my father have bread to spare, while I perish here with hunger?", and shall next arise and come to his father, and confess to him, saying, "I have sinned against heaven and before thee, and am not worthy to be called thy son; make me as one of thy hired servants."

When he shall thus confess, then he shall be counted worthy of more than he prayed for. For the father does not receive him as a hired servant, neither does he look upon him as a stranger, but he kisses him as a son, he brings him back to life as from the dead, and counts him worthy of the divine feast, and gives him his former and precious robe. So that, on this account, there is singing and gladness in the paternal home.

For this is the work of the Father's loving kindness and goodness, that not only should He make him alive from the dead, but that He should render his grace illustrious through the Spirit. Therefore, instead of corruption, He clothes him with an incorruptible garment; instead of hunger, He kills the fatted calf; instead of far journeys, the Father watched for his return, providing shoes for his feet; and, what is most wonderful, placed a divine signet-ring upon his hand; whilst by all these things He begat him afresh in the image of the glory of Christ.

Athanasius, Letter VII

Reflection Questions

- Why does Christ our true God, through our Church's readings, offer this story of the Prodigal Son at this time before the Great Fast?

- Do I appreciate the real meaning of responsible repentance?

- What demands will my sincere repentance ask of me, as I observe this pre-Lenten Sunday?

SUNDAY OF MEATFARE

Hegumen Nicholas

In your justice do not call me to judgment, scrutinizing my actions and correcting my misdeeds: in your mercy look not upon my transgressions, but save me, O God almighty.

Matins Canon, Ode 1

Readings

1 Corinthians 8:8-9:2

Matthew 25:31-46

Meditation

More properly this day is called the Sunday of the Last Judgment and the prayers in the Triodion for this day are prodigal with the images, culled from the prophets Daniel and Joel, of a fearful doomsday. We stand in this Josaphat Valley of judgment, before entering the Sacrament of the Great Fast. Through Moldavia, in the north of Romania, lie a scattered handful of unique artistic constructions, these are monastic Churches whose external walls were frescoed during the last part of the 16th century. The frescoes chart the hero figures and incidents of the long saga of the Church's history, including the taking of Constantinople in 1453.

But on the west wall history stops, and the artists display the final and ultimate moment of created time. The west wall was always left apart to depict the Last Judgment. Reading the Vespers and Matins services for this Sunday is akin to standing before that solemn representation, where the Trinity is seated on high and all creation, angelic and human, in varying guises and differing states of soul, throng and cluster in groups across the west wall. The scarlet river of Daniel's prophecy, snakes its way down through this gathering of joyful saints and despairing sinners. Every one of these monastic Churches has the crimson torrent as its most dramatic feature.

As the kontakion for the day puts it: "When you come with glory upon the world, all will tremble. The river of fire will transport all men before your tribunal. Then will the books be opened, and things long hidden be revealed. On that day snatch me from the unquenchable fire, and let me stand on your right hand, O Judge most just."

Icon of the Last Judgment

And yet in one way we do not wait for a final revelatory moment: daily we judge ourselves, and sense the eternal verdict even here and now. "I tremble and am fearful, censured by my own conscience." (*Ikos*) The fast of Lent – a communal and ecclesial sacrament, not a private feat of endurance – completes and perfects this self-knowledge. It sharply clears our eyes of falsehood and points up the simple reality of ourselves before God: that is the reality of repentance.

"O Savior and most just judge, pity me and snatch me from the fire of punishment, which justly I should undergo at the tribunal. Grant me remission before the end by right actions and repentance." (*Matins Canon, 8th Ode*) This is a prayer fit for any day of the calendar, sad or joyful, fast or feast. It shows our standing condition at all times: confident because repentant, living within the bright paschal mystery of the Church, yet aware of the dark possibilities of sin that paradoxically crowd around us until the moment of our death.

Not by any pre-constructed design, but by the customary haphazard chance of liturgical fabrication, the Sunday of the Last Judgment stands in the Triodion a week before the commencement of the Fast. But it can find an appropriate place at any season of the year, since it is our human situation: waiting for judgment. "The fire is ready, the worm is set in place. But also joy, glory, remission, light that knows no evening, the rejoicing of the just. Who will be able to escape the agony and enjoy the good things?" (*Matins Canon, Ode 9*) The judgment is one that offers rewards as well as punishments.

Year after year the people and the monastics of these Moldavian monasteries processed around the church, especially for the sorrowful Paschal procession before Easter Matins, and always passed the judgment fresco on the West Wall of their church. It proclaims its same message whatever the occasion of the feast, joyful or sad. The Service for Last Judgment in the Triodion does the same office for us: it points up our constant condition of waiting expectantly for the open manifestation of what we already know.

Patristic Reading

But it is right for us to be afraid of the second death, that which is full of weeping and gnashing of teeth, and of groanings and miseries, that which is situated in outer darkness. But blessed shall be the faithful and the righteous in that Resurrection, in which they expect to be awakened and to receive the good promises, made them. But as for the wicked who are not faithful, in the Resurrection woe to them, because of that which is laid up for them!

It would be better for them according to the faith which they possess, were they not to arise. For the servant, for whom his Lord is preparing stripes and bonds, while he is sleeping desires not to awake, for he knows that when the dawn shall have come and he shall awake, his Lord will scourge and bind him.

But the good servant, to whom his Lord has promised gifts, looks expectantly for the time when dawn shall come and he shall receive presents from his Lord. And even though he is soundly sleeping, in his dream he sees something like what his Lord is about to give him, whatsoever He has promised him, and he rejoices in his dream, and exults, and is gladdened. As for the wicked, his sleep is not pleasant to him, for he imagines that lo! the dawn has come for him, and his heart is broken in his dream.

Aphrahat, Select Demonstrations

Reflection Questions

- Because this Sunday stresses the notion of being prepared, "before the end", are we preparing ourselves by using the ever-present "now"?

- Are we spiritually prepared to undertake the physical fast that is recommended?

- Do we understand that a "true fast" includes the virtues and charity?

SUNDAY OF CHEESEFARE

Archpriest John G. Petro

Adam was banished from Paradise because of the forbidden fruit. He sat before the gate, sighing and lamenting: Alas! Woe is me! What is happening to me? I have transgressed the commandment of the Lord, and now I am deprived of every blessing. O Paradise, so delightful, you were planted for me; and now you are closed because of Eve. Beseech your creator who has also fashioned me to fill me with the fragrance of your flowers once again ...

Vespers Apostichon

Readings

Romans 13:11b – 14:4

Matthew 6:14-21

Meditation

Have you ever done something that you immediately regretted? Perhaps it was a harsh word said with little forethought, and as soon as the syllables escaped your mouth you realized how hurtful they were. Perhaps it was a foolish decision, and as soon as you acted upon it, you felt that sickening pain in the pit of your stomach. It is the pain that comes from the realization that we must now live with the consequences of our decisions.

Adam and Eve must have felt the same pain. When they sat outside the gates of Paradise and came to the full realization of what they had done, of what they had lost, the ache must have been overwhelming. They had been created for communion with God. They enjoyed, not only all the gifts of Paradise, but they especially enjoyed the life of deep union with their Creator.

The crafty Serpent, however, knew their deepest desires. He knew they wanted to be like God. So he deceived them by enticing them to eat the forbidden fruit. Now they sat outside the gates of Paradise, slumped over, head in hands, and they ached. They ached for all they had lost.

There is a bit of Adam and Eve in each of us. We too have been created for communion with God. We too long for a life of intimacy with our Creator. Yet we realize that we live far from this divine intimacy. Why is this?

Icon of the Expulsion from Paradise

The Serpent also knows our deepest longings. He knows the secrets of our hearts, our hopes and desires. As the master deceiver, he knows exactly how to mask evil and make it appear so appealing, so inviting, so good. Like Adam and Eve, we also take his bait; and as soon as we say yes to it, the Evil One unmasks it, and we again feel that awful feeling in the pit of our stomachs. Once again we have fallen; once again the saga of Adam and Eve is replicated in each of us.

Adam and Eve fell from Paradise because they did not fast. They allowed their appetites to rule them. We too have taken the bait and fallen. How do we return to Paradise? We do what Adam and Eve refused to do. We find our way back by fasting.

We now stand on the threshold of the Great Fast. We are about to enter the arena in which we do battle with the powers of evil within us. Let us embrace this holy Fast with confidence. Let us fast, not only from food, but also from all evil desires. God, who loves us, continues to work in us. Let us persevere for these next forty days.

Patristic Reading

What more? A noble thing is philanthropy, and the support of the poor, and the assistance of human weakness. Go forth a little way from the city, and behold the new city, the storehouse of piety, the common treasury of the wealthy, in which the superfluities of their wealth, aye, and even their necessaries, are stored, in consequence of his exhortations, freed from the power of the moth, no longer gladdening the eyes of the thief, and escaping both the emulation of envy, and the corruption of time: where disease is regarded in a religious light, and disaster is thought a blessing, and sympathy is put to the test.

Why should I compare with this work Thebes of the seven portals, and the Egyptian Thebes, and the walls of Babylon, and the Carian tomb of Mausolus, and the Pyramids, and the bronze without weight of Colossus, or the size and beauty of shrines that are no more, and all the other objects of men's wonder, and historic record, from which their founders gained no advantage, except a slight reward of fame? My subject is most wonderful of all, the short road to salvation, the easiest ascent to heaven. There is no longer before our eyes that terrible and piteous spectacle of men who are living corpses, the greater part of whose limbs have mortified, driven away from their cities and homes and public places and fountains, aye, and from their own dearest ones, recognizable by their names rather than by their features. They are no longer brought before us at our gatherings and meetings, in our common intercourse and union, no longer the objects of hatred, instead of pity on account of their disease; composers of piteous songs, if any of them have their voice still left to them. Why should I try to express in tragic style all our experiences, when no language can be adequate to their hard lot?

He, however it was, who took the lead in pressing upon those who were men, that they ought not to despise their fellowmen, not to dishonour Christ, the one Head of all, by their inhuman treatment of them; but to use the misfortunes of others as the opportunity of firmly establishing their own lot, and to lend to God that mercy of which they stand in need at his hands. He did not therefore disdain to honour with his lips this disease, noble and of noble ancestry and brilliant reputation though he was, but saluted them as brethren, not, as some might suppose, from vainglory, (for who was so far removed from this feeling?) but taking the lead in approaching to tend them, as a consequence of his philosophy, and so giving not only a speaking, but also a silent, instruction.

Gregory Nazianzen, the Panegyric on Basil

Reflection Questions

- As I look into the mirror of my soul, what is there within me that I would not want God to see?

- Even though change is difficult and sometimes hurts, how will I present this part of me to God?

- How do I plan to fast this year? How will my fasting allow God to work more fully in me?

LENTEN VESPERS

Steven Puluka

Vespers is the evening prayer of the Church, a tradition we owe to our Jewish forebears. Genesis tells us that the world began in darkness and became light, "evening and morning came, the first day" (*Genesis 1:5*) Vespers is the service performed ideally at sundown, with the singing of "O Joyful Light" happening as the sun disappears behind the horizon beginning the next day. Thus the singing of the prokeimenon following this hymn is the first singing for the new day.

This liturgical moment takes on a special character during the celebration of vespers on Sunday evenings of the Great Fast. Sunday is the weekly commemoration of the Resurrection, a mini-Pascha. During this day in the Great Fast we celebrate the Divine Liturgy and use all the normal Resurrectional tone music that we do throughout the year.

Weekdays during the Great Fast have a different tenor. We suspend the daily celebration of the Divine Liturgy as incompatible with the mood of *metanoia* (repentance) for the season. We shift from festive Resurectional melodies in a major key to solemn heart wrenching melodies in a minor key. We currently most frequently encounter these melodies during the Liturgy of the Presanctified Gifts.

Liturgically the shift between these two moods occurs at this moment of vespers on Sunday evening, as we leave Sunday with the singing of "O Joyful Light" and enter Monday with the special prokeimenon prescribed for this purpose by the Triodion (variable prayers special to the Great Fast).

Thus on Sunday evening we begin with a normal vespers service in the same key and melodies used throughout the year. But with the special prokeimenon we shift back into the Lenten melodies for the remainder of the service. During the rest of the week the entire service is sung to the Lenten melodies.

The prokeimenon and their verses are all taken from the Psalms. Throughout the year we sing the same Psalm verses every week with a certain collection for each day based on the liturgical theme of the day. During the Great Fast there are two special texts chosen for Sunday evening taken in alternate weeks.

Hide not your face from your servant, for I am in distress; answer quickly, come close to my soul and redeem me.

You have granted me the heritage, O God, of those who fear your name.

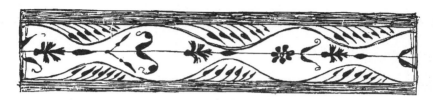

These capture the spirit of our Lenten journey. They capture the sense of *metanoia* and hope that characterizes the season of the Great Fast. They form the perfect launching pad for our next week of ascetical experiences.

Each weekday vespers service includes two readings from the Old Testament: Genesis and Proverbs. Each day has a specific prokeimenon for each of these readings. The structure is identical to how we take the epistle reading during the Divine Liturgy. Each of these Psalm selections matches the spirit of the reading and day.

A similar liturgical change happens during daily matins in the Great Fast. Here we replace the prokeimenon "The Lord is God" with the singing of the great Alleluia. In the same way that we shift the musical emphasis to a solemn tone that allows us to anticipate the joyful music of the Resurrection to come, we anticipate the coming of God in the Resurrection by singing Alleluia instead of the great affirmation of monotheism at matins.

This moment of matins corresponds with sunrise. Both vespers and matins are linking the sun to God. We affirm that the sun that was worshipped as a God in many cultures is but a symbol of our real one true God. We drop this monotheistic appellation during the Great Fast in order to more joyfully re-proclaim the message with Pascha.

Interestingly, both eastern and western Christian liturgy makes a change in singing Alleluia during matins of the Great Fast, but the changes are opposite. In the west they DROP the singing of Alleluia for the fast and resume singing it afterwards.

Another shift in vespers for the Great Fast occurs with the readings of sections of the Psalter (book of Psalms from the Bible). Outside of the Great Fast the entire Psalter is read at vespers and matins each week. The Psalter is divided into 20 roughly equal sections, called kathisma; two are read at matins, one at vespers, with none on Sunday evening. The bulk of the year this is simply a continuous reading with kathisma One on Saturday vespers and the rest in order at matins and vespers from there.

During the Great Fast the entire Psalter is read twice per week with additional sections being taken at the first, third, sixth and ninth hours in addition to matins and vespers. Sunday vespers is still without any kathisma assigned and Saturday evening, still the first. But the remainder are distributed thematically throughout the week. Vespers from Monday to Friday have the 18th kathisma assigned to them. This consists of the single Psalm 118 (119), the longest Psalm in the bible that extols learning the way of the Lord. This selection makes Psalm 118 (119) the theme Psalm for the season. Meditation on the ways of the Lord expressed here is obviously highly valued by the creators of our liturgical services. Prayerful reading of this Psalter and Psalm 118 (119) would be an especially fruitful practice during the Great Fast.

On Wednesday and Friday evenings we modify the Lenten vespers service to include communion. We can still recognize these structures of vespers, but the additions to support the communion aspect of the service create some unique features as well.

THE LITURGY OF THE PRESANCTIFIED GIFTS

Father Elias L. Rafaj

The Season of the Great Fast attempts to focus our mind, body and heart on the suffering and death of Jesus Christ and His glorious resurrection. The Church takes upon itself the gravity of the great mystery of our Lord's death and resurrection by using a more somber tone for the liturgical chant, by clothing itself in the colors of mourning (dark red and purple), by deep prostrations, Lenten prayers and by specific liturgical services that are celebrated only during the Great Fast.

The Liturgy of the Presanctified Gifts is one of these services, of ancient origin, used to mark the weekdays of the Great Fast, when no Divine Liturgy was celebrated. The Church saw in the celebration of the Eucharist the joyful witness to the resurrection of Jesus Christ. In the fourth century, the fathers decreed that the Eucharistic Liturgy would not be celebrated during the weekdays of the Great Fast because of the triumphant nature of the Divine Liturgy. The reserved Body of Christ was set aside (hence the name "presanctified") to be given to the faithful during the somber weekdays of the Fast. The Liturgy of the Presanctified Gifts gave strength to the faithful as they went through the difficult period of the Great Fast, week by week drawing closer to the drama of the passion and also to the glory of the Resurrection.

The Liturgy of the Presanctified Gifts is celebrated as an evening service, after a day of rigorous fasting and spiritual discipline befitting the holy season of the fast. A number of very specific actions take place in the Liturgy of the Presanctified Gifts:

- Lenten vespers
- Readings from the Old Testament Books of Genesis and Proverbs, reminding us of the static relationship between God and humankind
- Blessing with the lit candle, a reminder of the catechumens who are preparing for their baptism ("illumination") at Pascha
- The offering of incense in preparation of the procession with the Eucharistic Gifts
- Procession with the Gifts and the song of the entrance, beckoning us to draw strength from the Body of Christ and to become witnesses to Eternal Life
- Chanting of "Our Father" and Holy Communion

The Church provides encouragement for the faithful through participation in the Body of Christ received at the Presanctified Liturgy. The Great Fast, although very somber, is a period of reflection on the Mystery of our salvation, the new Passover. As we struggle to reorient our lives to God, so that we may fully share in this new Passover, we are given the Body of Jesus to help us in our weakness and bring us to the Resurrection.

SCOPE OF SCRIPTURE READINGS DURING THE GREAT FAST

Father James Spontak

The season of the Great Fast is filled with rich and varied themes and lessons that cannot adequately be represented by any one image or concept. Yet the notion of the Church as "on the way", journeying in a continual pilgrimage, captures something essential to the mood and purpose of this holy season of the year.

One element of greatfast worship and discipline which contributes to this experience of the pilgrim church is the cycle of readings selected from the Old Testament during the weekdays of the Great Forty-Days' Fast.

While the season of the Great Fast is itself an image of the journey of each person to his or her heavenly destiny, it also serves as the last link in a chain of typical events: the forty years of the Israelites' wandering in the desert, the forty-day march of Elijah to Mount Horeb and the forty-day fast of our Lord – each provide a symbolic and didactic basis for the forty days of the Great Fast.

An appreciation of the liturgical and penitential features of the Holy Great Fast, as well as of the accompanying meditations in this book, can thus be enriched by some awareness of the use of the Holy Bible and the selection of scriptural readings, particularly from the Old Testament, during the season of the Great Forty-Days' Fast.

In our Byzantine Catholic Church during the weekday greatfast liturgical services, specifically at the sixth hour and vespers, the continuous reading of Genesis, Isaiah, and Proverbs forms the cycle of greatfast weekday lessons. The pattern and content of this cycle of readings is evidence of that period when the Great Fast was still the principal pre-baptismal season of the Church. The catechetical character of greatfast services in their original context is an important feature for those who reflect upon these readings today. Thus, these selections are to be read and applied with an eye to a deepening and renewal of the Christian's baptismal commitment and of the life which flows from this holy mystery.

Each day at the sixth hour, which is one of the daily liturgical services designed for prayer at noontime – the middle of the day, the Church prescribes a reading from the *Book of Isaiah.* These Old Testament readings are known as paremias. Prominent in the late eighth century before Christ, and sensitive to the religious implications of the social and political events leading to the eventual fall of Jerusalem and the exile of its inhabitants, the Holy Prophet Isaiah constantly proclaims the message of trust and confidence in God.

Justice on the part of the people and their rulers and sincerity in divine worship are concerns are found repeatedly at the core of Isaiah's message. Besides the significance of the content of his message, the zeal and intensity of this man of God are a needed stimulus in carrying out any effort of renewal and repentance during the Holy Great Forty-Days' Fast.

During vespers, the Church's official evening liturgical service, there are readings selected daily from the books of Genesis and Proverbs. Many of the readings of Genesis present the fundamental truths upon which salvation rests, and thus deal with creation, the origin and destiny of humanity, the reality of sin, and the promise of redemption.

Other readings from Genesis are taken from the "patriarchal history" – the treasured memories of Abraham, Isaac, Jacob and Joseph. Besides displaying exemplary traits of faith, wisdom and virtue, these patriarchal narratives contain features that will prove to be typical of the events of the coming Redeemer and the salvation that He brings. In this regard, Joseph's words summarizing the course and outcome of the trying ordeal he experienced at the hands of his brothers are a hint of similar circumstances in the events of Jesus' life: "You meant evil against me; but God meant it for good, to bring it about that many people should be kept alive, as they are today." (*Genesis 50:20, sixth Friday of the Great Fast*)

Sections from the Book of Proverbs are also read at vespers. Often, the dominant tone of these collections of wise sayings is that of human, worldly wisdom. At the same time, there is also religious teaching. Thus, the recurring message is that God rewards truth, charity, purity of heart and humility, and punishes the contrary vices. Ultimately, all such virtues are based on wisdom, which amounts to a fear of God, a kind of ultimate trust in Him. It soon becomes obvious why the Book of Proverbs was incorporated the cycle of Greatfast readings, for it served as a primer of practical wisdom in daily life and offered moral instructions for the believer.

The epistle and Gospel readings prescribed for the Divine Liturgy on the Saturdays and Sundays of the Great Forty-Days' Fast are for the most part from the Epistle to the Hebrews and the Gospel of Mark. Once more, there is a continual reminder of the journey that is so characteristic of the Great Fast as well as of the patient yet taxing effort that is required of this pilgrim Church and its members. The Letter to the Hebrews portrays this sense of pilgrimage with its typology of the history of salvation, its illustration of Jesus as the Great High Priest, and its careful but vivid balance of promise and fulfillment as its central themes.

The Gospel of the Holy Evangelist Mark presents Jesus with decided clarity in terms of his role as a suffering Messiah, One Who invites his disciples to a way that will involve them in sharing the same destiny and end as their Lord.

The Church brings us to meet the Risen Christ Who is the destination of our Greatfast journey and acclaims Him as the "Great and Sacred Pasch, the Wisdom, Power and Word of God." (*Resurrection Matins Canon, Ode 9*) Coming to know Christ, the Word of God, by reading and reflecting upon the Sacred Scriptures during the season of the Great Fast is a reliable and effective means of making more vivid this vision of the Risen Lord and more fully realizing the joy of beholding his third-day Resurrection.

PRACTICAL INSIGHTS ON SAINT JOHN CLIMACUS

Marie C. Nester

Having gone up to heaven in the brightness of your virtues, and being firmly supported on solid ground, in faith, you have ascended in the boundlessness of contemplation; denouncing the tricks of demons, you have sheltered mortals from their misdeeds. O holy John, venerable ladder of virtues, intercede with the Lord to save his servants.

Sunday of St. John Climacus, Matins Sessional Hymn

Icon of Saint John Climacus

Saint John Climacus uses the image of a ladder to show us the way to heaven. He wants us to know the path is narrow and steep but not impossible to climb. We can climb that ladder if we stay focused on Jesus.

Staying focused also helps firefighters reach the top of their ladders. My husband and son, who are volunteer firefighters, tell me when they practice climbing ladders, they are told to stand erect and steady as they focus and look forward. We need to follow these same instructions when we think about climbing the ladder Saint John describes. We need to start each day by standing tall with our eyes looking forward to the kingdom of heaven.

Whenever I climb a steep ladder, I make sure someone is near to help me if I fall. Jesus knew we would need help as we climb our ladders to heaven. He gave us the Church and each other.

Yet, how easily I can forget to help someone else. Some days I get so busy trying to follow my own path that I do not notice someone who needs help. Those are the days I need to remember we must work together, just as firefighters, as we continue to climb.

This narrow ladder to heaven needs my full attention. Yet, some days I get distracted from the path I must follow. I'm busy worrying about my house, my job, and my family; and I forget to keep looking forward. Other days I worry about what everyone else is saying or doing, and I start to lose my balance. The only way I can keep on the path is by focusing on Jesus.

In his book The Ladder of Divine Ascent, Saint John Climacus describes how to keep our words, thoughts and actions focused on Jesus as we climb the ladder to heaven. Each day I look to Jesus and ask Him to guide my steps and keep my ladder balanced and steady as I climb closer to God.

With this in mind, we must strive to stay focused on Jesus even during busy daily activities. We also need to help other people who start to fall from their ladder to heaven. We must continue to fix our focus on Jesus throughout the year, with the same intensity that we have during the Great Fast.

Icon of Christ, the Bridegroom

THE PRAYER OF ST. EPHREM

O Lord and Master of my life,
    keep from me the spirit of indifference
    and discouragement,
        lust of power, and idle chatter.

Prostration

Instead, grant to me, Your servant,
    the spirit of wholeness of being,
        humble-mindedness, patience, and love.

Prostration

O Lord and King,
    grant me the grace to be aware of my sins
        and not to judge my brother and sister;
            for You are blessed,
                now and ever and forever. Amen.

Prostration

This beautiful penitential prayer is traditionally
prayed EACH DAY during the Great Fast.

THE FIRST MONDAY OF THE GREAT FAST

Father Gregory J. Noga

Wash yourselves; make yourselves clean; remove all evil of your doings ... learn to do good: seek justice; correct oppression ... though your sins are like scarlet, they shall be as white as wool."

Isaiah 1:16, 17a, 18

Readings

Isaiah 1:1-20

Genesis 1:1-13

Proverbs 1:1-20

Meditation

One can readily see from this excerpt of one of three readings for today, why this first day of the Great Fast is called Pure Monday. It is a clarion call to repentance, which is more than just saying "I'm sorry," and softly alludes to the day of our Baptism, Chrismation and Communication, when we "put on Christ". That is the day we were truly pure, innocent and Godlike; it was in a word, our "discipleship".

Discipleship, the action to "put on Christ", is a process of spiritual refining, a process that requires steadfastness and sometimes the chastening hand of God as the Book of Job manifests. In the Book of Proverbs, we are instructed that "the fear of the Lord is the beginning of knowledge; fools despise wisdom and instruction." (*Proverbs 1:7*) "Wisdom is a kindly spirit," Solomon teaches (*Proverbs 1:6*). Wisdom is therefore necessary to elude the artful temptations of evil and such wisdom is gained by becoming the servants of all men for the love of God, which is Discipleship.

A popular poster reads: "The journey of a thousand miles begins with the first step". The journey of the Great Fast is one of prayer, mortification, and almsgiving. The "first step" or primary component is prayer, both formal (matins, hours, vespers, compline) and informal (contemplation). Prayer requires quiet time and steadfastness. For those rediscovering our rich Tradition or those who are entering the Byzantine

Tradition for the first time, it is better to begin with ten-minute periods that remain focused rather than to try a full hour. Remember that the Great Fast is a journey and we have 40 days to complete that journey.

Secondly, someone once said that to achieve the realm of sainthood, all must be burned in the purifying crucible of mortification. Fasting allows one to juxtapose physical hunger and thirst for food, with spiritual hunger and thirst for God. It ought to be remembered, though, that our Tradition teaches that fasting, as a withdrawal from sinful activity, is the primary goal – not the elimination of food or substitution of one for another, e.g., non-dairy for dairy. Elimination is the operative word.

Come eagerly, O Faithful, with the firm armor of the Fast as a shield. Let us turn aside from every delusion of the enemy. Let us not be consumed by the gratification of our passions, nor fear the fire of temptations, for by them, Christ, the Lover of Mankind, will reward us with crowns for our patient endurance. Therefore, praying with trust let us bow before Him, praying for peace and abundant mercy for our souls.

Vespers, at Psalm 140

Finally, there is almsgiving. The degree, to which we sacrifice for God, so is the degree of glory with God. In other words, no sacrifice – no glory.

Reflection Questions

- What are my plans for prayer during this Great Fast? Am I setting aside quiet time? Planning to attend more of the Liturgical Hours as available in my parish?

- Do I keep the letter of the law with regard to fasting, or the spirit as well? Do I physically and spiritually experience the lack of that from which I have fasted?

- Do I plan to give alms during this Holy Season? Do I give out of my abundance, or out of my need?

THE FIRST TUESDAY OF THE GREAT FAST

Hegumen Leo R. Schlosser, O.S.B.

Be sober, O my soul, and keep watch; pour out your tears and sighs; let the Fast lighten the burden of your sins. By the zeal of repentance, avoid the fire of Hades, and by sorrow – for your failures, tear up the garment of sadness and receive from God the garment of joy.

Matins, 2nd Hymn, Ode 2

Readings

Isaiah 1:19 – 2:3

Genesis 1:14-23

Proverbs 1:20-33

Meditation

Prayer, Fasting and Almsgiving are the special tools of the Lenten Season that bring us light, and peace, and joy. Prayer ultimately is a deep abiding awareness of God. Prayer and sin are in opposition. Thus the ancient Fathers would define prayer as remembering God and Sin as forgetting God. We cannot commit sin in the presence of God. Sin is always a kind of forgetfulness. Sin is closing our eyes, our minds, and our hearts to the reality of God's presence.

Fasting is not dieting. Fasting is done for God. Dieting is done for me! Fasting is learning to make room for God. We do not live on bread alone, but on every word that comes from the mouth of God. Fasting allows us to identify with the poor, who are hungry – not because they are fasting, but because they are poor. Almsgiving is giving of my time, talent and treasures to those who are in need.

Thus, if my prayer is a deep abiding awareness of God, sin will have no place in my life.

If fasting is done for the right reason, then we will become aware of the needs of the poor, the lonely, those in prison, and those who are dying. Our prayer and our fasting should then lead to almsgiving.

The greatest of all alms is the gift of forgiveness. Our Lenten prayer and fasting begins with the Vespers of Mutual Forgiveness. Our Lenten observance must lead to the wonderful Kiss of Peace that we celebrate on Easter morning as we celebrate the Lord's victory over sin and death, and recognize Him in our brothers and sisters.

Easter joy is celebrating the Christ who is alive in the hearts of those who believe. Joy is the echo of God's life within us.

The Great Fast is a joyful season of fasting, taking time to be with and for God. It is a season of Alleluia – that is, praising God. The Great Fast is a time to recognize and praise God for his steadfast love manifested in the life, work, teaching and miracles of Jesus Christ.

During the days of Lent, we will add to the usual measure of our service something by way of private prayer and abstinence from food and drink, so that each of us will have something above the assigned measure to offer to God of his own will with the joy of the Holy Spirit.

Chapter 49, Rule of St. Benedict

Reflection Questions

- Do I often say my prayers without praying?
- Is prayer a priority in my daily life?
- Is my service to others an outgrowth of my prayer and fasting?
- Am I willing to share a gift of God's forgiveness with those who have hurt or offended me?

THE FIRST WEDNESDAY OF THE GREAT FAST

Father Robert M. Pipta

By fasting let us subdue the passions of our mind, and let us put on the wings of the spirit, so that overcoming the tempest raised by the Enemy, we may be worthy to adore the Cross of the Son of God. He willed to be sacrificed for the world, and we now spiritually keep the feast of his Resurrection from the dead. Let us ascend the mountain with the apostles to glorify the Son of the Father who loves all mankind, to whom all power is now given.

Matins Aposticha

Readings

Isaiah 2:3-11

Genesis 1:24 – 2:3

Proverbs 2:1-22

Meditation

When we hear the word "fasting", the first thought to enter our minds usually involves our being bound or restricted by this particular discipline of the Church. Immediately, we start to consider what we "can't have" or what we will "give up".

While we may call to mind some good works which might fill the void created by our abstinence, more often we seem to be tempted into considering various ways in which the prescriptions of the fast may be lightened for us.

Now that we have entered the first week of the Great Fast, let us move beyond this initial view of fasting and reflect upon fasting's true purpose – to set us free.

Fasting enables us to "put on the wings of the spirit." It sets to flight our true self, released from the bondage of the Devil. Indeed, it is a prescription, but one which we receive joyfully in order to be freed from the spiritual sickness which is sin.

Fasting accomplishes this by focusing our attention on the ultimate sustenance – life in our Lord Jesus Christ!

Jesus Christ came that we may have life and have it abundantly (*John 10:10*). His life was poured out for us on the Cross at Calvary and continues to be poured out for us in the mysteries of the Church. Our job is to embrace and partake of this life that we may ascend to the eternal kingdom of heaven.

A simple desire to be filled with all that our Lord Jesus Christ has shared with us is not enough. True desire leads to a willing and joyous self-emptying which makes room for the abundance of God's grace thus blotting out the stain of sin.

When we fast, thereby allowing room to be filled with God's grace, we are truly who we are created to be – free individuals in God's image and likeness.

Let us be clear about what truly binds us and Who truly sets us free.

Reflection Questions

- Do I thank God for this opportune and most solemn time of fasting?
- How well do I keep the Fast?
- In what areas can I grow in order to keep the Fast better?

THE FIRST THURSDAY OF THE GREAT FAST

Father Donald Valasek

Receiving the rays of purity, O my soul, be filled with light and leave the darkness of sin, so that the dawn of forgiveness may rise upon you in the Holy Spirit. Illumine my soul also, for it is clouded by evil.

Matins Canon, Ode 4

Readings

Isaiah 2:11-21

Genesis 2:4-19

Proverbs 3:1-18

Meditation

The first week of the Great Fast seems, to me, to be the most difficult of the Seven Weeks. The first week is the time that many of us, if not all of us, become serious with our fasting and abstaining. Once we decide why we are fasting and from what we are abstaining; that's when we want it the most – whether it be from food, places, things, and even people.

We are called during the first week of the Great Fast to look at fasting as our means to Spiritual Cleansing in order to rightly celebrate the Resurrection of Christ. The whole Season is a movement toward the Resurrection. While taking these forward steps, we try to become a little more perfect. We begin to realize how far we have strayed from the Lord. We slowly come to realize our need for forgiveness and we become aware of the Presence of God in our lives. "In all your ways be mindful of Him, and He will make straight your paths." (*Proverbs 3:6*)

We read in the Book of Genesis how God created humankind in His Image. "The Lord God formed man out of the clay of the ground, and blew into his nostrils the breath of life and so man became a living being." (*Genesis 2:7*) Over a period of time, we, through sin, have distorted that Image; disguised that Image, of God in us. By intensifying our prayers, fasting and charitable works, we slowly uncover or renew that Image of God in us.

The Great Fast is a Season of Re-creation. This is the time for us to become serious about our relationship with Jesus Christ. We have allowed many opportunities to pass us by, to reflect the Love of Christ to others.

Now is the time for us to pull back and take a realistic look at our relationship with God. He sees us as we are and knows what we need. "You know what each needs even before they ask or are aware of it". (*Vespers, Prayer of Light*) We must admit our shortcomings and be willing to make changes in our lives, as many as necessary, in order to allow Christ's Image to shine through us.

We must begin "one step at a time". "A journey of a thousand miles begins with a single step."

Reflection Questions

- Can I willingly admit my shortcomings to myself and to others?
- Am I willing to make changes in my personal life?
- Do I see a need to reflect the Image of Christ to others?

THE FIRST FRIDAY OF THE GREAT FAST

Sister Elaine Kisinko, O.S.B.M.

O Light of those who are in darkness, O Christ our Savior, salvation of the hopeless, I keep watch before You, O Prince of peace. Illumine me with your rays; I know no other God but You.

Matins Canon, Ode 5

Readings

Isaiah 3:1-14

Genesis 2:20 – 3:20

Proverbs 3:19-24

Meditation

Lord, I come before you today asking that at this time, I may pray in the light of your holy presence. Be with me now as we approach the completion of the first week of the fast. Help me to continue to walk with You and to come ever closer to You in the Lenten journey of the weeks ahead. As always, I thank You for all of your goodness and grace in my life and in the lives of everyone.

Truly does your light illuminate all that is good and holy in our lives. The physical world in which we live constantly reminds us of the contrast between light and darkness.

The difference between day and night, sunshine and cloudy days, the gray bleakness of winter and the brightness of summer, all reflect this division in the rhythm of our living.

Even on the days that are the brightest and sunniest, however, I must acknowledge the dark areas with which I struggle: my frustration when things aren't following "my plan"; my impatience when people don't live up to my expectations; the anger that I display and the futile worries I impose upon myself. I allow fear to enter my heart when my trust in You wavers. All of these prevent me from living as one who reflects your light as You have called me to do.

Help me to better remember that your light is the light that came into our world for us and the darkness overcame it not. The distractions, imperfections, blemishes, and trials of this life are always with me, but You remain my constant light – unwavering, unchanging, always available and accessible to penetrate all darkness. Illuminate and strengthen me, Lord, in your everlasting light until the day when I am with You in the complete and perfect splendor of your light and where darkness is no more.

Reflection Questions

- Can I find a practical positive way to help me when I find myself in shadow and darkness rather than in the Light of Christ?

- How can I better reflect his Light in my world?

- Are there new ways and places that I should seek in which to bring his Light?

THE FIRST SATURDAY OF THE GREAT FAST

Archpriest John Kudrick

The Sabbath was made for man, not man for the Sabbath.

Mark 2:27

Doctors very often advise diets, special kinds of food, or less food because dieting is good for our health. It is no wonder that God also prescribes this kind of cure for us.

Cardinal Lubachivsky

Readings

Hebrews 1:1-12

Mark 2:23 – 3:5

Meditation

The Great Fast should be approached as something that was made for us and not vice versa.

We must consider fasting as something that God has given to us for our own good and not as a burden or a challenge. We know that fasting brings us closer to that true and healthy relationship with God that He wills for us. There is a reason for fasting; it is not a punishment or a bitter medicine but a regimen for healthy living.

Prayer is an opportunity to communicate with our God, not an obligation. God intends prayer to be for our good: we were not made for prayer but prayer for us. The expanded schedule of liturgical services in our parishes during this season is intended to provide us with opportunities for growing in our love for God and for others through prayer and public worship.

We should consider almsgiving as an opportunity to share the hardships of others and to share with them our resources. Self-sacrifice is not a punishment for success; it is God's way of helping us to realize our interdependence with others.

During this first Great Fast week, we have attempted to purify ourselves spiritually. On this first Saturday, we commemorate the holy Greatmartyr Saint Theodore of Tyre. In the year 362 A.D., he encouraged the Christians of Tyre to subsist on boiled wheat throughout Pure Week rather than become defiled with foods which had been sprinkled with the blood of pagan sacrifices. Saint Theodore's dual examples of martyrdom (witness) and asceticism (prayer and fasting) are held up to us as sterling examples for us to emulate.

Reflection Questions

- Do we understand the Great Fast disciplines as helpful for our spiritual health?

- Does the example of St. Theodore motivate us to enter fully into the Great Fast?

THE FIRST SUNDAY OF THE GREAT FAST

Barbara Yastishock Lutz, Ed.D.

By nature You are beyond measure, O Lord; yet in these last times You deigned to accept the limitations of the flesh. By your incarnation You assumed all aspects of our human nature. We now inscribe the image of your likeness so that we might worthily venerate it, and that we might be raised up to your love from which we draw your great mercy, according to the tradition of your holy Apostles.

Vespers, at Psalm 140

Readings

- Hebrews **11**:24-26,32 **12**:2
- John 1:43-51

Meditation

Today is the first Sunday of the Great Fast, the Sunday of Holy Images.

It is time for the Divine Liturgy to begin. I rise as the Royal Doors open and bow to venerate the Holy Icons of Christ the Teacher and the Holy Theotokos as the priest or deacon incenses them. I ponder; Christ is central to these icons. Next, I bow my head as I, too, am incensed – as a holy image! But, am I really, really worthy to receive this honor?

You, O God, have created me to your image but what have I done and what am I doing to become your likeness? Is Christ central to my life? Is Christ evident in both my public and private lives, my thoughts, my words, my actions?

As I gaze upon the Holy Image of Christ the Teacher, its spirituality, its holiness, the radiance of peace and love captivate me. Whenever I come before this Icon, Christ is always blessing me. My heart can be filled with joy, my shoulders heavy with burdens, my eyes filled with tears, my soul burning with love – at all times Jesus is loving and blessing me!

What do others see when they look at me, when they really come to know me? Do they see an image of God, a likeness of Christ always ready and willing to be open to others? Do I rejoice with them, share their burdens, wipe their tears and be of service, through my love of God?

To write an icon, an iconographer prepares mentally and spiritually through prayer and fasting to transform an earthly canvas into a heavenly image.

During this Great Fast, through prayer, fasting, spiritual reading, reflection and good works, I, too, can transform my earthly canvas into a heavenly image – reflecting Christ as central in my life, worthy to be incensed.

As God sent His Son to become man, accepting the limitations of the flesh and assuming all aspects of our human nature, so, too, God invites all mankind to prevail over those limitations of the flesh and human nature and to become Godlike.

Create in me a new heart, O God, and renew a right spirit within me. From temptation, sin and evil, spare me, O Lord, and raise me up to your love from which we draw your great mercy.

Icon of the Holy Fathers of the Councils

Patristic Reading

When He who is a pure spirit, without form or limit, immeasurable in the boundlessness of his own nature, existing as God, takes upon Himself the form of a servant in substance and in stature, and a body of flesh, then you may draw his likeness, and show it to anyone willing to contemplate it. Depict his ineffable condescension, his virginal birth, his baptism in the Jordan, his transfiguration on Tabor, his all-powerful sufferings, his death and miracles, the proofs of his Godhead, the deeds which He worked in the flesh through divine power, his saving Cross, his Sepulchre, and Resurrection, and ascent into heaven. Give to it all the endurance of engraving and color. Have no fear or anxiety; worship is not all of the same kind.

Abraham worshipped the sons of Emmor, impious men in ignorance of God, when he bought the double cave for a tomb (*Genesis 23:7; Acts 7:16*). Jacob worshipped his brother Esau and Pharaoh, the Egyptian, but on the point of his staff (*Genesis 33:3*). He worshipped – he did not adore. Joshua and Daniel worshipped an angel of God (*Joshua 5:14*); they did not adore him. The worship of latreia is one thing, and the worship, which is given to merit [10] another. Now, as we are talking of images and worship, let us analyze the exact meaning of each. An image is a likeness of the original with a certain difference, for it is not an exact reproduction of the original. Thus, the Son is the living, substantial, unchangeable Image of the invisible God (*Colossians 1:15*), bearing in Himself the whole Father, being in all things equal to Him, differing only in being begotten by the Father, Who is the Begetter; the Son is begotten. The Father does not proceed from the Son, but the Son from the Father. It is through the Son, though not after Him, that He is what He is, the Father who generates. In God, too, there are representations and images of his future acts – that is to say – his counsel from all eternity, which is ever unchangeable. That which is divine is immutable; there is no change in Him, or shadow of change (*James 1:17*).

Blessed Denis, (the Carthusian [i.e., Pseudo-Dionysius]) who has made divine things in God's presence his study, says that these representations and images are marked out beforehand. In his counsels, God has noted and settled all that He would do, the unchanging future events before they came to pass. In the same way, a man who wished to build a house would first make and think out a plan. Again, visible things are images of invisible and intangible things, on which they throw a faint light. Holy Scripture clothes in figure God and the angels, and the same holy man (Blessed Denis) explains why.

When sensible things sufficiently render what is beyond sense, and give a form to what is intangible, a medium would be reckoned imperfect according to our standard, if it did not fully represent material vision, or if it required effort of mind.

If, therefore, Holy Scripture, providing for our need, ever putting before us what is intangible, clothes it in flesh, does it not make an image of what is thus invested with our nature, and brought to the level of our desires, yet invisible? A certain conception through the senses thus takes place in the brain, which was not there before, and is transmitted to the judicial faculty, and added to the mental store. Gregory, who is so eloquent about God, says that the mind, which is set upon getting beyond corporeal things, is incapable of doing it. For the invisible things of God since the creation of the world are made visible through images (*Romans 1:20*). We see images in creation which remind us faintly of God, as when, for instance, we speak of the holy and adorable Trinity, imaged by the sun, or light, or burning rays, or by a running fountain, or a full river, or by the mind, speech, or the spirit within us, or by a rose tree, or a sprouting flower, or a sweet fragrance.

Apologia of St. John Damascene Against Iconoclasts

Reflection Questions

- What do others see in me? Do they recognize the image and likeness of God?

- How can I transform myself, my earthly canvas, into a heavenly image?

- Is Christ really central to my whole life, in all I think, in all I say, in all I do?

THE SECOND MONDAY OF THE GREAT FAST

Jean Figel

The beginning of our salvation was announced by Gabriel to Mary. When the angel appeared to her, she did not refuse the greeting, she did not doubt as Sarah once did in the tent. Rather, she said: "Behold the handmaid of the Lord; let it be done to me according to your word."

Matins, Sessional Hymn III

Readings

Isaiah 4:2 – 5:6

Genesis 3:21 – 4:7

Proverbs 3:34 – 4:22

Meditation

As I begin the second week of the Great Fast, my thoughts linger on the annunciation by the angel Gabriel to the Blessed Mother Mary and her life as the mother of Jesus. I travel back many years when the doctor announced to me that I, too, would bear a child. I was blessed with this wondrous announcement three times, and so I can imagine how Mary felt when Gabriel appeared to her.

When I think of Jesus, I do not think first of the little boy in his mother's arms or the teenager learning to use a hammer with his loving father. I do not think of him as 12 years old. After he was discovered missing for three days, his parents found Him in the Temple and scolded Him. But He told them He was about his Father's business.

I'm sure our Blessed Mother faced some of the same problems I did in raising children. Many times, I've prayed to her for help and wondered how she solved the challenges of child-rearing in the days before disposable diapers, nursing bottles, toy cars, baby dolls, washing machines, etc.

As a parent, one of the most unbearable pains is to lose a child to death. What pain the Blessed Mother must have felt as she watched her son, Jesus, condemned to death, suffering as He carried his heavy cross on the road to Golgotha. The sword of sorrow surely pierced her heart when they threw her Son on the cross and simultaneously pounded three large heavy pointed nails into his hands and feet.

As she stood at the foot of the cross with the Apostle John, Jesus said, "'Woman, here is your son.' Then he said to the disciple, 'Here is your mother'." (*John 19:26-27*) When they removed Him from the cross, I can feel her pain and tears when she held Him in her arms as she did when He was a small boy.

When Jesus hung on the cross, He gave the Blessed Mother to us as our mother. Through her intercession with God, she is ready to protect and help us in our daily lives. She is our constant travel companion on our journey Home to our Heavenly Father.

May the Theotokos intercede with her Son for all of us sinners. "Let my prayer ascend to You like incense." (*Psalm 140:3; Liturgy of the Presanctified Gifts*)

Reflection Questions

- Do I accept adversities of life according to God's will as our Blessed Mother did ("Behold the handmaid of the Lord") or do I want only answers according to my will?

- Do I remember to pray to the Theotokos, who, as the mother of Jesus, will intercede for me for the salvation of my soul?

- Through prayer and fasting, can I forgive the offenses of others, so that my sins may be forgiven?

THE SECOND TUESDAY OF THE GREAT FAST

Sister Mary Virginia Ermay, O. Carm.

O Word of God, my Lord Jesus Christ, I am lost in the wilderness of my transgressions: call me back to You. I am keeping away from You because of my sins: draw me back to You. I am dead: revive me. Let my Lent be for me an occasion to shed tears that will cleanse me. I cry out to You: "O Christ my Lord, have mercy on me, for You are gracious and generous in your mercy."

Vespers Sticheron

Readings

Isaiah 5:7-16

Genesis 4:8-15

Proverbs 5:1-15

Meditation

With heartfelt understanding let us make these words of Scripture our own. We have transgressed; we have given little heed to the love lavished on us by our loving Savior. We have gone away from Him. He waits for us. He awaits our return without complaining – with a love that knows no limit.

We are busy with lots of nice people, nice movies and places, nice books, parties, food, games. All are lovely, good and healthy in themselves. Yet, sometimes these gradually take us away from our time with God, limiting the time and quality of attention we give Him in return for His great Love.

This is the second week of the Great Fast; I may need to arrange or rearrange more quiet time with God. Maybe I can also visit with a friend who would welcome a good word for the Great Fast, or someone on my street who is lonely. An elderly person whom I know may welcome some help, company or a prayer companion. I can also offer to take someone to Church on Sunday.

Yes Lord, I have heard your Word and I want to try. Help me, whom You love so much. Help me to get closer to You during this Great Fast. O Holy Mother of God, save me.

Reflection Questions

- Have I given enough thought to my Great Fast disposition?

- Have I made any real changes? If not, how can I help myself to begin?

- Have I really grasped the greatness of God's love for me?

- Can I get closer to Him? Do I want to? How would this affect my life?

THE SECOND WEDNESDAY OF THE GREAT FAST

Lector Jack Figel, Deacon Candidate

O apostles of Christ who shine your light on all mortals, you are the treasuries of the holy knowledge of God. Through your prayers deliver from temptation those who praise you. Guide us successfully through the course of this Fast; direct our lives in peace, so that with our eyes lifted up to the Passion of Christ, we may with courage give praise to our God.

Vespers, Stichera at Psalm 140

Readings

Isaiah 5:16-25

Genesis 4:16-26

Proverbs 5:15 – 6:3

Meditation

Each time we participate in Vespers or the Presanctified Liturgy, there is a point when a dramatic event takes place. After singing the stichera (or propers) of the day with Psalm 140, the clergy process around the altar and through the iconostasis, similar to the entrance with the Gospel during the Divine Liturgy. After proclaiming "Wisdom! Be attentive!" the people sing the Hymn of the Evening – "O Joyful Light!" – and the altar, the people and the entire church are incensed.

For dramatic effect, the church lights should be brightened at this time, symbolizing the lighting of the lamps in the Temple, and the entrance of Christ into the world as the new light. This shift in emphasis from the darkness to the light demonstrates how Christ's Incarnation and Resurrection – the whole story of salvation history – is real and present for us yesterday, today and tomorrow.

This lighting of the lamps (or brightening of the light bulbs!) is in sharp contrast to the darkening of the world around us as the sun drops below the horizon and evening comes. Even though the visible sun is slowly waning, we welcome Christ into the world to keep the spiritual light shining in our lives.

The light of Christ is also spread throughout the world – first by the apostles, then by the martyrs and saints, and now by each one of us who is baptized into Christ. We received the light at our baptism and it has grown within us as we discovered the faith. We all have the responsibility to share that light with the world and to make Christ present in the world. The light of Christ that we all carry is manifest or realized by the way we live our life each day. The kindness we share with others around us, those we meet on the street or in the shopping mall, or even those with whom we might contact through e-mail, is the true light of Christ spreading throughout the world. Our behavior demonstrates the fact that we are Christians and that we follow the teachings of our Lord and Savior.

The Great Fast is not only a time for penance and fasting, but also for "doing good works". During this period the prayers and liturgical services of the Byzantine Church remind us to not only reflect on the things we have done wrong that we wish to change, but more importantly, on the things we should do right in our daily lives. Do we say hello to our neighbor on the street? Do we give loving hugs to our spouses or children each morning as they go off to work or school? Do we compliment co-workers when they do a good job? Do we give others the right-of-way on the street as we drive our car? Do we help elderly with getting groceries in the store? Do we help fellow students in school when they have trouble with their locker? Do we constantly let Christ "shine" into the world by our actions – do we live a Christian life?

Let us all be more diligent in our daily life to let the light of Christ shine through us into the world just as the lights shine more brightly in church when we sing "O Joyful Light!"

Reflection Questions

- How do we let the light of Christ shine in us to others with whom we interact every day?

- Have we learned to be true Christians and live according to his commandments and teachings?

- Do we live the Gospel of Jesus Christ each day, or only on Sundays when we come to church?

THE SECOND THURSDAY OF THE GREAT FAST

Sebastian Carnazzo

Your side was pierced when You were hanging on the wood of the cross; but by coming down, You fashioned life for me; I had been deadened by the evil of the Serpent who showed me the forbidden fruit. Therefore, O Christ, I glorify You and implore Your compassion: grant that I may complete the course of the Fast with contrition and adore Your Passion and holy Resurrection.

Vespers at Psalm 140

Readings

Isaiah 6:1-12

Genesis 5:1-24

Proverbs 6:3-20

Meditation

The first Fast was from the fruit of the Tree of Knowledge.

Like Eve standing before the Tree of Knowledge, gazing upon its tantalizing fruit while conversing with the deceitful Serpent, so is the Christian, the bride of Christ, every time we contemplate a sinful deed. Our holy father in the Faith, St. John Chrysostom, while commenting on Genesis said that there was no excuse for the woman to have been speaking to the Serpent in the first place. Rather she should have been conversing "with the person for whose sake she came into being, with whom she shared everything on equal terms, and whose helpmate she had been made." (*Sixteenth Homily, 5*)

If Eve had been doing that for which she had been created, she would never have encountered the Serpent in the first place. Likewise, we Christians would never encounter the occasion of sin if we only did that for which we were re-created in the waters of Baptism, converse with the Person for whose sake we came into being, with whom we share everything on equal terms, and whose helpmate we have been made.

As Eve was the bride of Adam, so we Christians are the "bride of Christ" (*Ephesians 5:21-23*). Just as Eve would not have fallen had she been conversing with Adam instead of the Serpent, so we cannot fall as long as we remain in conversation with Christ our Bridegroom. Learning a lesson from blessed Peter, who only began to sink in the waters when he took his eyes off of our Lord, let us keep our eyes focused on Him, crying out "Lord save me!" Let us learn from the example of the good thief, who in the depths of his suffering on his own cross, remained focused on his Creator, and say with him, "Lord remember me when You come into your kingdom!"

During this wonderful gift of the Great Fast, as we prepare for the coming of our Bridegroom, may we remember the words of the prophet, "How long will you lie there, O sluggard? When will you arise from your sleep? Give your eyes no sleep and your eyelids no slumber; save yourself like a gazelle from the hunter, like a bird from the hand of the fowler." (*Proverbs 6:9, 4-5*) Let us keep our lamps filled and our wicks trimmed. Let us stand with our Holy Mother and the beloved disciple in the Garden of Eden, at the foot of the cross, the tree of life, gazing upon our Savior, "as the pleasing cluster of the true Vine" (*Sessional Hymn II*), waiting to partake in the Holy Inebriation.

Then we will be ready when He comes, heralded by "thousands of archangels, tens of thousands of angels ... Singing, shouting, crying out and saying the triumphal hymn: 'Holy, holy, holy is the Lord of hosts, ... Blessed is He Who comes in the name of the Lord ...'." (*Divine Liturgy of St. John Chrysostom*) Like Enoch, who walked with God, we will enter with our Bridegroom into the heavenly marriage banquet, feast on the Bread of Heaven and drink of the Fruit of the Vine (*Genesis 5:24; Hebrews 11:5; Jude 14-16*). We will see with our eyes, and hear with our ears, and understand with our hearts. The angels will say to us, "Behold this has touched your lips, and shall take away your iniquities, and shall cleanse your sins." (*Isaiah 6:1-12*)

Reflection Questions

- What in my life am I reordering in order to better fix my eyes on Jesus?
- How am I preparing for the Bridegroom's arrival?

THE SECOND FRIDAY OF THE GREAT FAST

Dana Tomcanin

O my soul, abstain from evil, find your pleasure in divine love. Open your door to all the virtues, and by self-renunciation and prayer, close the door to sin. Save me, O Lord, from condemnation: for I am stained with evil passions and darkened by sin.

Matins Canon, Ode 9

Readings

Isaiah 7:1-14a

Genesis 5:32 – 6:8

Proverbs 6:20 – 7:1

Meditation

Every year during the season of the Great Fast we pause to reflect on where we are in our life's journey and where we want to be. Over and over, all the prayers and readings remind us to abstain from evil, close the door to sin, go beyond earthly passions and become more Christlike. One of the greatest evils which we are continually warned against in the penitential prayer of St. Ephrem, is the sin of idle talk.

What is idle talk? It is the wickedness of words devoid of meaning and purpose. The gospels say "men will render account for every careless word they utter." (*Matthew 12:36*)

The ability to think and speak – to express ourselves – is one of God's greatest gifts to us. It is what sets us apart from plants and animals. It is what shows us to be made in the image and likeness of God. God calls Himself "the Word", saying in the Gospel "In the beginning was the Word and the Word was with God and the Word was God". (*John 1:1*)

With words we can give thanks, create goodness, beauty and wisdom. But these same words can curse, gossip, lie and condemn. The same tongue that sings praises to God can also criticize and blaspheme.

We must continually strive to control what we say. St. John Climacus says that "he who has become aware of his sins has controlled his tongue, but a talkative person has yet to know himself as he ought," since "he who cares for his salvation cuts down on words, while he who gains repentance shuns talkativeness like fire." (Saint John Climacus, *Ladder of Divine Ascent*, Step 11: On Talkativeness and Silence)

The Book of Proverbs is filled with teachings about words and silence. "A soft answer turns away wrath, but a harsh word stirs up anger. The tongue of the wise dispenses knowledge, but the mouths of fools pour out folly. The eyes of the Lord are on every place, keeping watch on the evil and the good. A gentle tongue is a tree of life, but perverseness in it breaks the spirit." (*Proverbs 15:1-14*)

May we use this season of the Great Fast as a time to understand how we ourselves use words and control our tongue as we pray during the Presanctified Liturgy: "Set a guard O Lord about my mouth and a portal around my lips."

Reflection Questions

- Have I spoken without thinking, or spoken too much, or spoken anything that is impure, or shameless, or without need or order, or unreasonable or unclean?
- Have I thought or said angry words or foul words?
- Have I spread rumors or gossiped in thought or word?
- Have I ridiculed people in thought, word or action? Have I mocked others in a harmful way? Have I insulted anyone?

THE SECOND ALL SOULS SATURDAY

Anthony Dragani

The abyss of passions opens before me as a tempest of enemies surrounding me. Hasten to save me, O Savior God, as you delivered the prophet from the sea monster.

Matins Canon, Ode 6

Readings

Hebrews 3:12-16

Mark 1:35-44

Meditation

As we journey deeper into the Great Fast, we will come to experience an interior struggle – provided that we take this journey seriously. Spiritual exercises, such as fasting and even prayer, are challenging for us. Indeed, they can appear almost strenuous. They seem at times to go against our very nature. This is because we are in the midst of a "war" with our passions.

In the early centuries of Christianity, making a decision to follow Jesus could frequently result in martyrdom. Christianity was an illegal religion, and those who joined the Church often paid with their lives. Hence, everyone was well aware that being a Christian was a very serious commitment, not to be made by the lighthearted. Christianity was synonymous with persecution and struggle.

This situation changed dramatically in the fourth century, when the Emperor St. Constantine became a Christian and legalized the religion. Many of the wealthiest nobles and merchants joined the Church in an attempt to win the emperor's favor. The struggle appeared to be over, and one could comfortably be a Christian without any great effort.

Many women and men, however, longed for a deeper spirituality. They realized that a spiritual life absent of struggle was ultimately hollow and fruitless. They moved to the desert, and began a serious battle with their passions. They found excessive desires for food, wealth, entertainment and sex to be the most difficult adversaries to overcome. In order to triumph over these longings, these men and women learned to call upon the mercy of the Lord day and night. These were the first monks.

During the Great Fast, each one of us is called to follow in the footsteps of these early monks, no matter what our state in life may be. Day after day, night after night, we must come face to face with our passions – our desires for more food, more sex, more money, and more leisure than we truly need. These desires threaten our spiritual well being, and if left unchecked will eventually devour us, much like the prophet Jonah was swallowed whole by the sea beast.

Sometimes, it may seem that the beast has already devoured us. When faced with the temptation to overindulge our appetites, we must follow the example of Jonah and call upon the mercy of the Lord to save us. The monks discovered that no enticement is so powerful that we cannot eventually pray it away. This is the struggle that we are called to engage in during this season of preparation, and with much prayer we may emerge from it with a whole new sense of spiritual well being.

Lord Jesus Christ, Son of the Living God, have mercy on me, a sinner!

Reflection Questions

- Am I making a serious effort to keep the fast, or am I barely keeping the minimum requirements?
- When faced with temptation, do I ask the Lord for assistance?

THE SECOND SUNDAY OF THE GREAT FAST

Betty J. Mowery

... He said to the paralyzed man, "I command you: Stand up! Pick up your mat and go home." The man stood and picked up his mat and went outside in the sight of everyone. They were awestruck: all gave praise to God, saying, "We have never seen anything like this!"

Mark 2:10b-12

Readings

Hebrews 1:10 – 2:3

Mark 2:1-12

Meditation

As I pressed with the crowd into the little house in the town of Capernaum, my heart was racing as I got closer to the one I desired to see – his name is Jesus. Just as I was about to reach out and touch Jesus, the thatching of the roof seemed to be breaking apart. Before we knew what was happening, a palsied man's friends lowered him down through a hole in the roof, right to the feet of Jesus!

Everyone became still, waiting for Jesus to heal the man. Much to our surprise, Jesus turns to the palsied man and says, "Son, your sins are forgiven." Where's the healing? What does He mean, "your sins are forgiven"?

As Jesus looked into our faces, He knew what we were thinking: "Who can forgive sins, but God only?" Quietly, He says, "Why is it troubling you that I say his sins are forgiven. Is it easier to say take up your mat and walk? But I say this so that you know that the Son of Man has the power on earth to forgive."

He then turns to the man and says, "Pick up your mat and go home." The man immediately arose, took up his mat and left. As the man left, all of us were amazed. We never heard or saw anything like this.

As I stood in awe at what we all had just witnessed, I thought of what Jesus had said, "your sins are forgiven." I began to realize the burden of sin in our hearts. The weight of sin that can be so overpowering that it paralyzes one more than a physical paralysis. Then I thought of the great news and the comfort Jesus had just shown us – by the grace of God our sins are forgiven. Jesus had come into this world to free us from our sins.

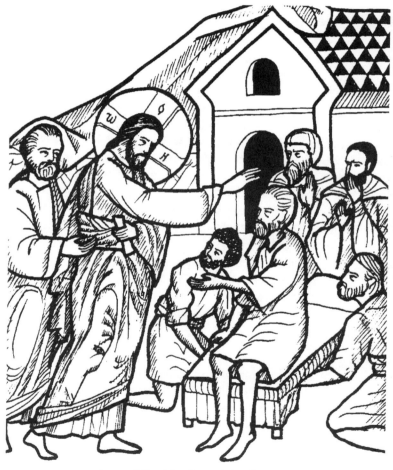

Icon of the Healing of the Paralytic

The faith and trust in Jesus as shown by the palsied man's friends, shows us that we, too, must have faith and trust in Jesus. We must also remember that Jesus showed us spiritual healing is very vital to the physical healing of our bodies.

As we journey through the Great Fast, may we be reminded that Jesus wants us to be free from sin. Let us lighten our burdens by casting away our sin to follow the path of Jesus.

Patristic Reading

The soul's death sentence, brought into effect by man's transgression, was in accord with the Creator's justice; for when our forefathers forsook God and chose to do their own will, He abandoned them, not subjecting them to constraint. And, for the reasons we have stated above, God in his compassion had already forewarned them of this sentence (*Genesis 2:17*). But in the abyss of his wisdom and the superabundance of his compassion He forbore and delayed in executing the sentence of death upon the body; and when He did pronounce it He relegated its execution to the future. He did not say to Adam, "Return whence you were taken", but "You are earth, and to earth you will return." (*Genesis 3:19*) Those who listen to these words with intelligence can gather from them that God did not make death (*Wisdom 1:13*), neither that of the soul nor that of the body. He did not originally give the command, "Die on the day you eat of it." (*Genesis 2:17*) Nor did He say, "Return now to earth," but "You will return." (*Genesis 3:19*) This He said as a forewarning, but He then delayed its just execution, without prejudicing the eventual outcome.

Death was thus to become the lot of our forefathers, just as it lies in store for us who are now living, and our body was rendered mortal. Death is thus a kind of protracted process or, rather, there are myriad of deaths, one death succeeding the next until we reach the one final and long-enduring death. For we are born into corruption, and having once come into existence we are in a state of transiency until we cease from this constant passing away and coming to be. We are never truly the same, although we may appear to be so to those who do not observe us closely. Just as a flame that catches at one end of the slender reed changes continually, and its existence is measured by the length of the reed, so we likewise are ever changing, and our measure is the length of life appointed to each of us.

That we should not be entirely ignorant of the superabundance of his compassion for us and the abyss of his wisdom, God deferred man's death, allowing him to live for a considerably longer time. From the first God shows that his discipline is merciful or, rather, that He delays a just chastisement so that we do not utterly despair. He granted time for repentance and for a new life pleasing to Him, while through the succession of generations He eased the sorrow produced by death.

Gregory Palamas, Topics of Natural and Theological Science

Reflection Questions

- In what ways have I put my faith and trust in Jesus?
- What are the times in my life when I can remember repenting, confessing my sins and knowing that my burdens were lifted?
- How can I increase my desire to follow in the path of Jesus?

THE THIRD MONDAY OF THE GREAT FAST

William J. Kress

O people, let us sing praise to our God who works wonders, for
He drew Israel out of slavery.

Matins Canon, Ode 1

Readings

Isaiah 8:13 – 9:6

Genesis 6:9-22

Proverbs 8:1-21

Meditation

During the course of the Great Fast, we are reminded of our
slavery caused by sin. Today the matins prayers mention that we should
sing praise to our God who works wonders, for He drew Israel out of
slavery. Our God does the same for us through Jesus, who draws us out
of slavery by dying for our sins. But do we really ever think about this
miracle and how it occurs daily in our lives?

The ancient Israelites understood and could see and feel their
slavery, but in this Modern Age, sometimes we do not even realize that
we are slaves at all. We go about our lives as Modern Man or Woman
doing whatever we do to survive and get by in this world. Often it
involves sins of various kinds that sometimes we do not even realize we
commit, until we later review our day's activities – if we do happen to
do a review. We need to realize that we are sinners and, as today's theme
suggests, turn to Fasting and Repentance.

The first ode goes on further to say: "O God, who has mercy on sinners, receive my tears of repentance, I have foolishly wasted my life. Listen to my cry. I have sinned; there is no need of anyone to accuse me, for I am ashamed of my actions."

Within ode eight of matins we say: "The Fast is our marvelous treasure and paternal inheritance, it is the mother of all those who serve Christ: let us find our joy in it, O faithful. It gives strength to our bodies, and it enlightens our spirits and our hearts."

This week of the Fast leads up to the Sunday of the Veneration of the Holy Cross, the source of our salvation. The ancient Israelites were led by fire to freedom; this light was a prefigurement of the Cross of Christ. Christ's death on the Cross is the source of our salvation, and his Resurrection, our life. Let us prepare for the celebration of the Holy Cross this Sunday and the effect it is meant to have on our lives by reflecting on the fact that Christ, the Son of God, died for us sinners.

Reflection Questions

- Do I view Fasting as a treasure or just a chore?

- Do I take some time to consider fasting, as the ode above suggests, as a source of strength?

- Do I ever take time to reflect on the day's activities and repent for any sins?

THE THIRD TUESDAY OF THE GREAT FAST

John Montalvo III

Let us purify ourselves by prayer and fasting, and let us serve God by caring for the poor. Let us weep and lament, for behold, this is the time to repent, so that we might escape the eternal sorrow in the fires of Gehenna. may glory be rendered to Christ who offers repentance to all mortals who are converted in the purity of their heart.

Matins, Sessional Hymn II

Readings

Isaiah 9:9 – 10:4

Genesis 7:1-5

Proverbs 8:23 – 9:11

Meditation

Prayer, fasting and caring for the poor – these expressions of our faith have come to characterize the season of the Great Fast. No matter what our background, each of us, even from our early childhood, realizes that these spiritual exercises prepare us for Pascha. As children we may recall the more frequent attendance of the liturgical services, especially the All Soul's Saturday Liturgies and the Liturgy of the Presanctified Gifts. We all have stories of what foods we would "give up" for the Great Fast. Some of us may even have saved spare change for the poor box or brought canned goods for the parish food pantry. While these types of expressions are indeed noble and praiseworthy for children as an introduction to our life in Christ, they are not particularly suited for mature Christian adults.

The extended liturgical services provide us, as the Body of Christ, with the opportunity to deepen our level of communication with God. The various prayers of the Lenten Triodion not only allow us to address God, but as we listen to the words of our communal prayers, they provide instruction in this very life we share with God and the community of faith. Our liturgical services are the banquet table that feeds our personal prayer.

As we follow the Lenten fast, we should understand that fasting is neither a punishment nor a burden. Rather, fasting has a spiritual dimension. Fasting allows us to control the desires of our fallen nature. In a manner of speaking, fasting causes a reversal of the misfortune produced by the eating of Adam and Eve. Whereas Adam and Eve are led out of the Paradise of Eden as a result of eating, the Church is led to the Paradise of Pascha by way of fasting.

Not to be overlooked, caring for the poor allows us to have a direct impact upon those less fortunate than ourselves and to put our faith in action. Caring for the poor is the direct response of our prayer and fasting. The text states that we serve God by caring for the poor. Although many of us see our contributions to the food pantry or the Saint Vincent de Paul Society as caring for the poor, the Gospel actually challenges us to make this more personal. True care for the poor requires each of us to personally minister.

In addition to our financial contributions, we should also contribute our time. By directly interacting with the poor, we imitate Christ who dwelt among us (*John 1:14*). We can accomplish this by volunteering at a homeless shelter or a food bank. Perhaps it is providing a meal to a person searching through a trash dumpster. Perhaps it is providing a meal to the sick and infirm of the neighborhood or parish.

The Great Fast provides us with the time to purify ourselves in order to serve God better. As adults, we must be willing to grow beyond the practices of our youth.

Consider the following questions along the journey, and as you do, allow this journey through the Great Fast to be a life changing experience for yourself and for those with whom you come in contact, all the while focusing on Christ, "who offers repentance to all mortals who are converted in the purity of heart."

Reflection Questions

- Do I allow the Lenten services to influence my prayer life?
- Do I view fasting as a burden or as a means to free myself from the desires of the flesh?
- How can I directly and personally minister to the poor?

THE THIRD WEDNESDAY OF THE GREAT FAST

Sister Ruth Plante, O.S.B.M.

I trust in the goodness of God forever and ever.

v. I will thank you forevermore; for this is your doing.

Prokeimenon, Liturgy of Presanctified Gifts

Readings

Isaiah 10:12-20

Genesis 7:6-9

Proverbs 9:12-18

Meditation

Day follows day, week follows week ... Each one holding a bounty of blessings and graced hours. Each one likewise holds a measure of challenge, struggle and pain. As I face the dawn and promise of each new day, it is also important that I reflect upon the goodness of the God who offers it to me sanctified by His suffering and death.

This week I see placed before me the holy and life-giving Cross. It serves as a reminder that I was redeemed at a great price – a price that was endured because of unconditional love. In Matins I pray: "Your word upholds the universe, O Christ, and for me, You endured the buffeting, spitting and crucifixion; I praise the greatness of your love forever." (*Canon, Ode 8*)

As I encounter each new day, recalling the love of Jesus can serve to build up my trust that all will be well. Perhaps everything will not fall into place according to my own plan, but trust in the goodness of the Lord enables me to let go of the need to control every facet of my life. I can then place the various events, questions, and problems into the hands of Jesus.

I know He loves me; I know all is his doing; I know I can look forward to the eternal life, which is promised to me through the death and Resurrection of Jesus.

Reflection Questions

- Do I truly recognize and appreciate the graces and blessings that are mine each day?

- As I look upon the Cross, am I mindful of the unconditional love that Jesus has for me?

- Do I see the loving hand of Jesus in everyone and everything that is a part of my life?

Icon of Saint Gregory Palamas

THE THIRD THURSDAY OF THE GREAT FAST

Bishop Basil M. Schott, O.F.M., D.D.

O Savior, You are the true sweetness who of old sweetened the bitterness of the waters of Marah, and by the wood you prefigured your divine Cross.

Vespers at Psalm 140

Readings

Isaiah 11:10 – 12:2

Genesis 7:11 – 8:4

Proverbs 10:1-22

Meditation

During the Great Fast we are continually reminded of the journey from darkness to light, which takes place in each of our lives. "O Cross of Christ, you are our light, the sacred insignia and the sign of victory: be the sweetness of our fasting, and make us worthy to bow before you."(*Matins Canon, Ode 9, third Wednesday of the Great Fast*)

The Cross is given to us as an aid to travel the ocean of the Great Fast to the shores of the Resurrection. Each of us is invited by the Church to use this acceptable time "to leave the darkness of sin and have the light of the dawn of forgiveness rise upon us." (*Matins Canon, Ode 4, first Thursday of the Great Fast*)

But how can our fasting be sweet? How can we shine with the light of charity and bow down in prayer?

Physical fasting is not the same as dieting, although often we achieve the same results, namely, the loss of weight. We are asked to give up certain foods in order to cleanse our bodies and as penance for our sins. Fasting is not exclusively concerned about food. "The true fast is the love of God, fervor in prayer, tears of contrition and concern for the poor and needy." (*Matins Canon, Ode 1, second Monday of the Great Fast*)

We are to shine with the light of charity and almsgiving. It is always easy to give from our bounty, but so difficult from our need.

Charity certainly includes material things, but also much more. Alms-giving or charity is multi-faceted. We need the power of the Cross to help us explore all the components of this praiseworthy work. We participate in spiritual almsgiving by being kind, gentle, forgiving, considerate, non-manipulative, supportive and not frozen in our own opinions and thoughts. However, sometimes our own reservoir of kindness, gentleness and forgiveness is at a very low level. It is precisely then that we are asked to share the little we have. Remember the widow's mite (*Luke 21:1-4*).

We are called to bow in prayer. We are called to participate in the Liturgy of the Presanctified Gifts and other prayer services in our parishes during the weekdays of the Great Fast. We participate in the services for the dead on the prescribed days and on Saturdays and on Sundays we rejoice in the celebration of the Divine Liturgy. We are also called to pray privately. One praiseworthy custom is the praying of the Psalms.

Finally, it essential for us to take the opportunities for prayer that God provides for us during the day – driving to work, waiting for an appointment, being on hold on the phone, or simply sitting down for quiet time. These are also wonderful opportunities for listening to God.

Prayer, fasting and almsgiving are needed as our constant companions on the journey to the shore of the Resurrection. On our own, we cannot accomplish much in the spiritual realm. But with the help of God – Father, Son and Holy Spirit – all things are possible.

Reflection Questions

- Have I set aside time each day to pray a Psalm and reflect upon its meaning in my life?

- Do I make good use of the opportunities for quiet time and listen to what God may be saying to me?

THE THIRD FRIDAY OF THE GREAT FAST

Father Michael Jude Wytish

O Savior, melt the hard rock of my heart; in your goodness, grant me the divine streams of compunction

Matins Canon, Ode 9

Readings

Isaiah 13:2-13

Genesis 8:4-21

Proverbs 10:31 – 11:12

Meditation

Have you ever found yourself putting things off until "tomorrow"? If so, you know that tomorrow never really seems to be the right time and whatever it is that you planned to do slips away into that vast pile of things you were supposed to do "tomorrow".

The same is often true in our spiritual journey. We usually start out with the best of intentions, but little by little, our fervor slips away or our attention is drawn elsewhere. We mean to get back to our journey; it's just a matter of "when".

Today we find ourselves rapidly approaching the mid-point of the Great Fast and we need to pause and ask "How far have we come on the road to repentance?" Have these days, thus far, been fruitful for us in our spiritual journey? Have we begun only to fall off course, or do our hearts still remain hard, closed to conversion and repentance?

One of the most difficult challenges for us is to admit that we are not perfect. We all would like to think that we've reached our goals. We like to think that there is no need for self-improvement. But if we are honest with ourselves we know that this is far from true.

There is no shame in acknowledging that we are not where we would like to be in our journey. In fact, no matter how far we progress, we know that there is always room for improvement. It would be a shame, however, if we were to choose to do nothing to better our situation.

Our intentions are usually very good, but in this case, good intentions are not enough. We must make these intentions concrete by living in such a way that our actions bring us closer to God. How can we be filled with joy on the day of the Resurrection if we have not experienced the hunger and longing that has preceded it? How can we celebrate the victory of Christ if we have not participated in the battle?

The days are indeed slipping by quickly, but it is never too late to begin. If we have come to this day and have realized that our journey has been halted, then let us do something about it. Take strength from the Cross that will be placed before our eyes this Sunday and set out on the road to the Resurrection.

After all, it is not how swiftly we begin the race that is important, but that we are able to cross the finish line and receive the crown of victory.

Reflection Questions

- Have I put off until "tomorrow" the spiritual practices that should have been begun yesterday?
- Am I where I would like to be in my journey toward Christ?
- What concrete steps can I take to bring myself closer to where I should be on the road to salvation?

THE THIRD SATURDAY OF THE GREAT FAST

Maureen M. Daddona, Ph.D.

In the furnace, the youths trampled the flames as they praised God; in their fervor, they chanted: Bless the Lord, all you works of the Lord.

Matins Canon, Ode 8

Readings

Hebrews 10:31-38

Mark 2:14-17

Meditation

The room was quiet, clam, peaceful. Rose petal softness floated in the air. His family sat, gently sobbing in their seat. Their loss would be difficult to face, but not impossible. At twenty-four years of age, his death came as an unexpected shock.

Then in the stillness, a voice rose. A melody of chant lifting the people to their feet in song, proclaiming the glory of God and the saving grace of the Trinity.

How strange it must seem to those who possess no awareness of the Lord: for those who have no concept of the Father's great love for his people; for those who lack any knowledge of the great sacrifice Christ made on our behalf; for those who have not experienced the all-encompassing power of the Holy Spirit in their lives.

How bewildering it must appear to them to hear singing and acclamations in a time of deep pain.

But not so for us, who sing with confidence, even in times of sorrow, proclaiming the wonders of our God: for us who stand with a strength born of an enduring faith in the promise and certainty of salvation.

"We would have you be clear about those who sleep in death; otherwise you might yield to grief, like those who have no hope." (*1 Thessalonians 4:13*)

Live as a child of hope, always aware that our God is the great lover of mankind. He brings us to a place of light, joy and peace. And we will sing the glory of the Resurrection unceasingly.

Reflection Questions

- Have I pondered that by Christ's death He trampled death, and now death itself – though a sorrowful loss of a loved one – is in fact, as absurd as our singing praise to God may seem at a funeral Liturgy or Panachida?

- Has the glorious Light of the Resurrection transformed my fear of death to hope in glory?

- Have I, in my prayers for departed ancestors, been thankful for the gift of faith they passed on through my family, and eventually, to me?

THE THIRD SUNDAY OF THE GREAT FAST

Sister Barbara Swindells, O.S.B.M.

Today we see the precious Cross of Christ placed before us; let us venerate it in joy as we bow before it; and let us beseech the Lord who was crucified on it, that He may grant us the grace to contemplate his holy and glorious Resurrection.

Matins, Hymn of Light

Readings

Hebrews 4:14 – 5:6

Mark 8:34 – 9:1

Meditation

Today, as I gaze upon the Cross, I see it first of all as an instrument of Christ's humiliation; of his rejection, even by his closest friends; of the pain and suffering caused by these as well as the physical suffering He endured; and of his eventual death.

My thoughts race back to those times in my life when I, too, felt humiliated and rejected. I know I did not always accept these crosses and often asked that they be removed. I am aware more and more of the pain and suffering in my own life and in the lives of people around me. Am I more ready to accept these crosses as a part of sharing in the mystery of the Passion of Christ?

But wait, there is more. This is only half of the Paschal mystery. I am called to venerate the Cross in joy, to go beyond the mystery of Christ's passion to the mystery of the Resurrection. Through the Cross, Jesus became a forgiving victim revealing a God who is self-giving, compassionate and loving. Jesus died on the Cross to transform all humankind and me.

After his death on the Cross, Jesus arose, not only alive, but also changed. He revealed a different way of living, a way of transformation. What then does this mean for me?

Everywhere I turn, I see a world where war and violence lurk around every corner; where so many people no longer respect life, especially that of the unborn and the elderly; where there is less and less concern about the environment and preserving it for future generations. I see a society that is more interested in personal gain and winning regardless of the cost and youth too often ready to give up or give in to what they perceive as hopeless situations.

The mystery of the Cross redefines the human element. It is about being the victory instead of just winning. It is refusing to hate or humiliate others. It is the way to nonviolence.

I cannot transform the world or even a small segment of society. However, I can begin to transform myself, or rather to allow Christ to work his transformation through me. Jesus asks that we follow Him on the journey to transformation. Not just to preach Jesus, but to become Jesus. I am not sure how this can be done. All I can do is get out of the way and let the mystery of the Cross transform me.

Patristic Reading

With those who live in the world and are associated with the material things that feed the passions, the demons wage war through practical activities; while with those who dwell in the wilderness, where material things are rare, they fight by troubling them with evil thoughts. This second mode of warfare is far more difficult to cope with; for warfare through things requires a specific time and place, and a fit occasion, whereas warfare of the intellect is mercurial and hard to control. But as our trusty weapon in this incorporeal fight we have been given pure prayer: that is why we are told to pray without ceasing (*1 Thessalonians 5:17*). Prayer strengthens the intellect in the struggle, since it can be practiced even without the body taking part.

With reference to the perfect mortification of the passions Paul says: "They that are Christ's have crucified the flesh together with the passions and desires." (*Galatians 5:24*) For when we mortify the passions, utterly destroy desires, and subjugate the will of the flesh to the Spirit, we take up the cross and follow Christ (*Matthew 16:24*). For withdrawal from the world is nothing else but the mortification of the passions and the manifestation of the life that is hidden in Christ (*Colossians 3:3-4*).

Theodoros the Great Ascetic, A Century of Spiritual Texts

Reflection Questions

- How do I look upon the Cross – as a mystery of the Passion or of the Resurrection?

- Am I ready to let Jesus transform me?

- What can I do to bring about change in my own life?

Icon of Christ showing the Way

THE FOURTH MONDAY OF THE GREAT FAST

Msgr. John T. Sekellick, J.C.L.

On this day let us bow before the Cross and all say joyfully: Rejoice, new tree of life. Rejoice, scepter of Christ our King. Rejoice, heavenly glory of humankind. Rejoice, strength of our faith. Rejoice, invincible trophy. Rejoice, vanquisher of the Enemy. Rejoice, radiance of brightness. Rejoice, glory of martyrs. Rejoice, strength of the just and holy ones. Rejoice, splendor of angels. Rejoice, holy Cross of the Lord.

Vespers at Psalm 140

Readings

Isaiah 14:24-32

Genesis 8:21 – 9:7

Proverbs 11:19 – 12:6

Meditation

Nestled in the northeast corner of Lackawanna County (PA) can be found the small borough of Jessup, (population 4,619). It is the home to six churches – five of which are Catholic, including Holy Ghost Byzantine parish, of which I have been Pastor since mid-September, 1999. Holy Ghost Church is situated on the hilltop where Church Street intersects with First Avenue. Its three golden domes topped with our traditional 3-bar cross dominate the skyline of the town and are visible from many points as one approaches Jessup from any direction. Those distinctive crosses made it easy for me to find the church when I moved from St. Mary's in Wilkes-Barre to serve in Jessup.

This week our Liturgy places the holy Cross of our Lord in the center of our churches to bring into focus and dominate, as it were, our movement through this Holy Season of the Great Fast (Lent). Without this focal point, our Lenten journey may become disoriented; we may find ourselves straying from our chosen spiritual goal. This week gives us an opportunity to set our sights on the distinguishing symbol of our salvation – assuredly our ultimate eternal goal.

The Cross is the means of our redemption and the unfathomable mystery of God's unique love. On the Cross, man and God meet. Sinfulness and holiness are brought together. Life and death are fastened to it. Hope and despair hang in its balance. Sorrow and joy, suffering and happiness, love and hate – each meet at the Cross.

Christ's salvific death on the Cross that gives us everlasting life remains one of the impenetrable mysteries of faith. We will never completely grasp God's plan involving us in this very mystery. Our eternal destiny depends upon the Cross. All of us have contributed to the tragedy of the crucifixion, to the suffering and death of Jesus by our own personal sinfulness. Yet, through the Cross, Christ has gained for us new life without pain, sorrow or sadness.

In the Cross we are also given partnership with Him as we carry our own burden of trial, need or personal anguish. When St. Paul wrote to the Galatians, he told them (and us): "I am crucified with Christ. It is no longer I that live, but Christ in me!" (*Galatians 2:20*) The Cross keeps the value of suffering in focus for us; the Cross gives meaning to the place of penance in today's sophisticated and dissipated world.

To stand under Jesus' Cross is a soul-shaking experience because we are vividly reminded of our own responsibility for moral failure and offenses against the holiness of God. We cannot skirt around the Cross casually because the Person on it has brought us forgiveness and hope. Behind its agony shines a promise: a victory won and a future assured. There is peace at the Cross which nobody will be able to disturb or remove from us. Through the Cross, heaven has been opened again to us. The Cross lifts us up into the arms of God.

Reflection Questions

- When I place myself at the feet of Christ crucified, am I awestruck by His sacrifice? Overwhelmed by a sense of personal sin?

- Am I grateful for this act of merciful love? Am I amazed at how He turned a seeming act full of despair into eternal victory over sin and death, the Source of all our hope?

THE FOURTH TUESDAY OF THE GREAT FAST

Paul Simko, Deacon Candidate, and wife, Sandy Simko

On this day at the midpoint of the Fast, let us faithfully prostrate ourselves before your Cross, which is planted in the middle of creation, O Word of God, Messiah and Mediator, as we also pray to see your Resurrection.

Matins Canon, Ode 2

Readings

Isaiah 25:1-9

Genesis 9:8-17

Proverbs 12:8-22

Meditation

As we begin the second half of our Lenten journey, it is time to pause and reflect on what we have accomplished leading to the Sunday of the Precious Cross. Following Meatfare and Cheesefare Sundays, we entered into the Great Fast vowing to control our worldly desires by fasting and prayer. We planned to visit with Christ more often by participating in the Lenten services.

On the Sunday of Orthodoxy, we were called upon to approach the Holy Icons, which would help strengthen our resolve and aid us in approaching God. Through the icons, we would join the saints, our intercessors with Christ our Messiah and Mediator.

By the Third Sunday of the Great Fast, we were able to approach the Precious Cross of our Lord knowing that it is the gateway to glory and the weapon through which we can stand against the demons that assail us in today's world.

We are at the midpoint of the Great Fast, willingly prostrating ourselves before the Precious Cross of our Lord. It is time to evaluate how our journey with Christ has been progressing: Has our Lenten season been one of fasting and prayer, walking with Christ while uniting our journey with his, or have we been too busy with the cares of this world? Has our fast been one of just watching what enters our mouth while carrying on with life as usual?

St. John Chrysostom reminds us: "For a true fast, you cannot fast only with your mouth. You must fast with your eyes, your ears, your feet, your hands, and all parts of your body." (*Third Homily*)

Do we feel too weary to continue onward? If so, let us look to Christ for the strength to continue our journey with Him. Let us visit with Him as much as possible in prayer, repentance and thanksgiving. We cannot be indifferent and let Him proceed to Golgotha alone while we continue in an attempt to follow a path of our own making.

It is time to renew our resolve, gather our energy and continue our journey with Christ. As we look toward the completion of the Great Fast, the Ladder of St. John Climacus is ahead to guide us and Holy Mary of Egypt stands before us to serve as our example in overcoming the passions of the world.

Let us not weaken in our Lenten devotion, but resolve with the aid of the Holy Spirit to continue our journey bearing our cross with Christ as He bears our sins.

When we finally reach the top of the hill, and approach, with bended knees, Christ on the Cross, we must realize that it isn't the end of the journey. It is just the beginning. For we must look beyond the Cross to the Resurrection and our new life in Christ – to the forgiveness of our sins and to our rebirth as adopted children of God.

Reflection Questions

- Has our Lenten journey been a faithful one of self-sacrifice or self-indulgence?

- Have we truly prostrated ourselves before the Cross of Christ or are we just going through the motions?

- Have we joined Christ on his way to Golgotha or are we standing back watching from a distance in fear of the "Pharisees" of today's world?

THE FOURTH WEDNESDAY OF THE GREAT FAST

Sister Carol Petrasovich, O.S.B.M.

Purified by fasting, come let us embrace with love the Cross of the Lord which is set before us; it is the treasure of power and holiness; in it, we ever praise Christ.

Matins, Odes 8

Readings

Isaiah 26:21 – 27:9

Genesis 9:18 – 10:1

Proverbs 12:23 – 13:9

Meditation

I wonder how many people, when reflecting upon the Cross of the Lord, view it as a treasure.

The word "treasure" usually connotes something precious and cherished, something valuable, perhaps even priceless.

In the same vein, how many of us think of the Cross as a symbol of suffering, something we must endure, a symbol of pain and death?

If we view the Cross of Jesus only as a symbol of his suffering and death, we miss the point.

During this fourth week of the Great Fast the Church sets the Cross before us as a symbol of hope and encouragement. It is set before us to give meaning to our lives: to give us life, strength and courage to persevere on the journey to the Resurrection. It is set before us to remind us of how much Jesus loved and continues to love. Ultimately, the cross is life and love.

Today, we are invited to embrace the Cross with love – to treasure its meaning. We are invited to reflect upon the power of the Cross, which is love, and the suffering that comes from truly loving.

Today the power that flows from the Cross gives meaning to our fasting. It enables us to enter the spiritual desert of our heart: to refocus, to look deeply within to where we have veered off course. It is instrumental in helping us to examine our attitude: to realize our need to repent, to forgive, to reconcile. It reminds us that each of us is in need of repentance and healing; that each of us is called to transformation. Today, Christ's Cross gives us strength to continue our journey.

As we venerate the Cross, let us do so with a sense of reverence and awe. Let us remember the gift of love that Jesus gave us through his death and Resurrection. Let us remember that to love wholeheartedly as Jesus did means that, at times, we may be called to surrender our way of life and allow it to be shaped by others. As we venerate the Cross, let us cherish it and give thanks and praise to the Lord who gave us victory over sin and death.

Reflection Questions

- How do I view the Cross? Is it a treasure? Or is it a source of healing, life and love?

- What areas of my life do I need to bring before the Cross for healing/transformation during the Great Fast?

- When we suffer because we love, the suffering has meaning. How do I embrace the "crosses" of my life?

THE FOURTH THURSDAY OF THE GREAT FAST

Sister Jean Marie Cihota, O.S.B.M.

Learn this lesson from the Lord, O my soul, for your sake He humbled himself even to death on the Cross: Exaltation humiliates but humility exalts. Do not become arrogant because of your good deeds ... Remembering your sins with a contrite and humble heart, say to the Lord ... Have mercy on me a sinner, O God, have mercy on me.

Vespers Aposticha

Readings

Isaiah 28:14-22

Genesis 10:32 – 11:9

Proverbs 13:19 – 14:6

Meditation

Today we continue to reflect upon the Cross of our Lord and Savior, Jesus Christ. During Matins we pray, "Seeing your Holy Cross exposed on this day, O Lord, we come forward and kiss it in faith ... learn this lesson from the Lord, O my soul, for your sake He humbled himself even to death on the Cross ... exaltation humiliates, but humility exalts."

What a contrast to the reading during Vespers (*Genesis 10:32 – 11:9*) in which the story of the Tower of Babel is unfolded. An arrogant people attempted to build a tower to reach the heavens! Their pride and arrogance led only to confusion, frustration and babble.

What motivated these people of Babel, who were intent on reaching to the heavens? What were the attitudes implanted in their hearts and minds? Was it a sense of pride? Was it arrogant hearts? Was it an extreme need to control others? Even an attempt to control God? Was it a lack of trust in our God, who comes down to transform our lives and bring us back to Him? Was it a dependence on their own strengths and abilities, rather than upon their God? Whatever the striving, it ultimately led to death and destruction!

But look to the Cross! What a contrast of images! The Cross seems demeaning, lowly and an ultimate humiliation. And yet, we know that through the Cross comes new life. Through humiliation comes exaltation. Through letting go comes fullness of life. Through death comes life. This is the gift of Himself and the ultimate gift of Love, freely given to each of us. Can we embrace the Cross? Can we accept the gift of Love that is offered to us?

As the tower of Babel peaked higher and higher, all were focused on "making it to the top". Their eyes were fixed on reaching the peak ahead, even if it meant stepping on others in the process.

Let our eyes rather gaze upon the Cross. Let us fix our eyes upon our God, and bow low before the precious Cross of our God.

"O faithful, let us go forth in love, and in thanksgiving bow low before the Cross of our God: for the Cross is the companion of those who keep vigil and the strength of those who fast." (*Matins Canon, Ode 1*)

Reflection Questions

- What are the towers of Babel that I attempt to build?
- What are the walls that I build in an attempt to keep God at a distance?
- How do I embrace the cross of everyday living and dying?

THE FOURTH FRIDAY OF THE GREAT FAST

Kevin E. Marks, Seminarian

Having received the privilege of beholding and venerating your holy Cross with joy, we now entreat You, O God our Savior, to enable us to behold your holy Passion. Strengthened through fasting, we bow low and praise the spear, the sponge and the reed of your crucifixion, which have delivered us from death and returned us to the delights of our life in Paradise. In thanksgiving we glorify You.

Vespers Sticheron at Psalm 140

Readings

Isaiah 29:13-23

Genesis 12:1-7

Proverbs 14:15-26

Meditation

The Holy Cross which we have been venerating this past week is now solemnly removed from the tetrapod. During this mid-point of the Great Fast season, the Cross enabled me to draw from its source of strength which finds its victory in the Radiant Resurrection of Jesus. We now prepare for the Fourth Sunday of this sacred penitential season meditating upon the meaning of the Life-Creating Cross of our Lord.

In the above liturgical text, some of the instruments of the passion are named: the spear, used to pierce the side of Christ; the sponge, given to Him on the Cross as he thirsted; and the reed, placed in his hand as the Roman soldiers humiliated and mocked him.

As I ponder on these sacred instruments of crucifixion, they help me to recall all that Jesus endured for the sake of my salvation. Being directed to venerate the spear, sponge and reed, these holy relics remind me of the origin of holiness which they touched, namely the Source of Life, that is Christ. It is not these instruments in themselves that bring me to Paradise, but Christ himself through his salvific action. For this, I glorify the King of Glory.

Approaching the Fourth Sunday of the Great Fast, let us use this Fourth Friday to take the time to be thankful for the Cross of the Lord, for it truly pours out the love Jesus has for us. Let us meditate on these instruments of the passion, for Christ subjected himself freely in all humility to them. Within this second half, let us take our Great Fast devotions and practices a step higher, or even, if we have fallen, to begin anew.

Through perseverance in prayer, fasting and almsgiving, may we ever be ready to walk with the Lord vicariously, awaiting Holy Week. Let us endure the passion and death with Him and anticipate that glorious and bright day of his Radiant Resurrection.

Reflection Questions

- What did the Holy Cross mean to me this past week as it was placed on the tetrapod and is now solemnly removed?

- How do I reflect upon the meaning of the instruments of the passion?

- Am I still achieving my Great Fast goals and continuing my Great Fast practices?

THE FOURTH SATURDAY OF THE GREAT FAST

Helen Soltis

Our soul waits for the Lord, Who is our help and our shield, for in Him our hearts rejoice; in his holy name we trust. May your kindness, O Lord, be upon us who have put our hope in You.

Psalm 33:20-22

Readings

Hebrews 6:9-12

Mark 7:31-37

Meditation

We are halfway through the journey of the Great Fast. We place our hope in the Lord, that He hears our prayers and supplications. Take a moment and reflect upon the past few weeks of our "journey of preparation".

We are given an opportunity to prepare ourselves through our prayers and fasting to deepen our personal relationship with God and to prepare for his eternal reward in heaven. Today we commemorate the souls of those who are asleep in the Lord "in the hope of resurrection and eternal life". Today, as we celebrate the Liturgy for the souls of the faithfully departed, we are mindful of our mortality and place our trust in the Lord, "Who is our help and our shield."

As we reflect upon our progress during Great Fast, we reflect upon those who have gone before us. During the Lenten journey, five Saturdays are designated to remember these souls. Today we offer prayers for the souls of members of our families, members of the congregation and benefactors, asking God to grant them mercy.

We pray for the departed with gratitude, for as they lived, they showed us how to live a life of prayer and fasting to prepare for our meeting with our Heavenly Father. By their dying, they showed us how to die with the expectation of being welcomed into God's presence. As we pray for their souls, we should become more aware of the journey of life and where it ends, and for our fervent desire for an eternal life in heaven.

These liturgical services, a departure from the presanctified services, offer an opportunity for us to reflect on our mortality and strive to become better Christians. Our time on earth is but a blink of an eye measured in eternity and a very short time to prepare to meet our Eternal Father.

We place our hope and trust in the Lord as we prepare ourselves through fasting and prayer. Fasting should not be viewed or undertaken as an obligation. It is, instead, a way of cleansing our body – coupled with prayer to cleanse our souls. These two devotions help bring us closer to God. Our challenge in this journey is to run the course of the fast without yielding to temptation and without failing in our human desires. By fasting, we are reminded of the emptiness of our body that we will be filled with the grace and glory of God through his love and kindness.

Today, remember those who have fallen asleep in the Lord. The memory of their death reminds us of our own mortality and this memory guides us in renewing our faith and trust in God. For "the purpose of Lent is precisely to recover the Christian meaning of time as preparation and pilgrimage." (Alexander Schmemann, *Great Lent Journey to Pascha*, St. Vladimir's Seminary Press, 1974)

Reflection Questions

- Am I putting forth my best effort by fasting and prayer to renew my faith and relationship with God?

- How can I strive to be a better Christian?

- If I were to be called by the Lord today, how do I think I would be judged?

THE FOURTH SUNDAY OF THE GREAT FAST

Father Thomas J. Loya

Having passed half the distance of this holy Fast, let us hasten to its completion in joy; let us anoint our souls with oil for the struggle, that we may worthy to venerate the holy Passion of Christ our God and to contemplate his glorious Resurrection.

Vespers at Psalm 140, Tone 7

Readings

Hebrews 6:13-20

Mark 9:17-31

Meditation

It is with a certain urgency that the Church puts before our eyes on this Fourth Sunday of the Great Fast, the example of St. John Climacus. This great penitential season is rapidly running its course. Our participation in the ultimate mystery that lies just ahead of us, Christ's suffering, death and Resurrection, cannot be approached with any superficiality. We have only a brief chance to renew or perhaps even to finally begin the serious ascetical disciplines exemplified by the life and writings of St. John Climacus.

In his book, "The Ladder of Divine Ascent", St. John presents to us the "renunciation of our lives" as the first rung of the ladder leading to our spiritual perfection. How urgent and relevant is John's message for us personally at this stage in the Great Fast and also as citizens living in the current era of time.

Renounce our lives? Die to ourselves? Our world programs us in the opposite direction, making narcissism a virtue: "My feelings", "I'm offended", "My rights", or "It's your fault" carries over to Church: "Liturgy is too long," "Church is too far," "I'm too hot/cold" or "I like this priest better than that one".

We have become a people of gargantuan pride, of egos that know no boundaries. Life, Church, other people, dare we say even Almighty God, must be on my terms according to my agenda or else.

I will let everyone know of my misery and demands by my incessant whining. I will file a lawsuit.

Icon of the Ladder of Saint John Climacus

Say "NO" to myself? This is a spiritual stripping of gears. Yet, without annihilating our false selves and allowing more silence in our lives, we cannot grow in holiness, and therefore in happiness. Our experience of the mysteries of Great Friday and Pascha will not be real. The marvelous and exciting sacramental life of the Church will continue to be nothing but a bore, as will our marriages, friendships, jobs and our lives in general.

The example of St. John Climacus is urgent in yet another respect. St. John renounced the world and gave himself to Christ at the age of 16. We often forget that throughout salvation history and the history of the Church, when God wanted to get the job done, He went to a young person. The examples of this are legion. The Most Holy Mother of God is the first among these many examples.

Today, while adults seem helpless to do anything but placate young people and the marketing world cleverly strives to steal the souls of young people, St. John Climacus stands as one of those many proofs of the grand potential of young people.

Let us challenge young people to be genuinely rebellious. Rebel against the narcissism of the world and truly stand apart by embracing the example of people like St. John Climacus. Become a true radical, a true standout – become a saint.

St. John's ladder of Divine Ascent begins with the renunciation of our lives. The top rung of his ladder is "love" – an "inebriation of the soul". Love's distinctive character is to be "a fountain of faith, an abyss of patience and a sea of humility". Let us make haste to climb St. John's ladder in these waning days of the Great Fast so that we might come to know real Love and truly rejoice in the Resurrection of Christ.

Patristic Reading

Step Five – On Penitence

Repentance is the renewal of baptism and is a contract with God for a fresh start in life. Repentance goes shopping for humility and is ever distrustful of bodily comfort. Repentance is critical awareness and sure watch over oneself. Repentance is the daughter of hope and the refusal to despair. (The penitent stands guilty – but undisgraced.) Repentance is reconciliation with the Lord by the performance of good deeds, which are the opposites of the sins. It is the purification of conscience and the voluntary endurance of affliction. The penitent deals out his own punishment, for repentance is the fierce persecution of the stomach and the flogging of the soul into intense awareness.

Come; gather round, listen here and I will speak to all of you who have angered the Lord. Crowd around me and see what He has revealed to my soul for your edification.

Let us give first place to the story of the dishonored workers – who still earned respect. Let us listen, take heed and act – we who may have suffered an unexpected fall. Rise up and be seated, all you who have been laid low by your sins. Hear what I have to say brothers. Listen, all you who long to be reconciled with God again in a true conversion.

I, the weakling, heard that there was a great and strange way of life and lowliness for those living in a separate monastery called "The Prison". It was under the authority of that man, that light of lights, referred to above, and during my visit I asked the good man to let me see it. This great man, who wished never to cause grief to any soul, gave his permission.

I went therefore to the abode of penitents, to that place of true grief, and if I may be so bold as to say so, I actually saw what the eye of inattentive man never saw, what the ear of the lackadaisical man never heard, what never entered the heart of a sluggard (*1 Corinthians 2:9*). I saw things done and said that could only draw down the mercy of God, deeds and attitudes of body that quickly win his love for men...

I saw there humble and contrite souls who were saddened by the weight of their burden. The stones themselves would have been moved to pity by their voices and by their cries to God. Looking down to the ground, they would say this: "We know, we know that we deserve every punishment and every torment. Rightly so. How could we make up for all that we owe, even if we had the entire world there to weep for us? All we ask, all we pray for, all we implore, is that in your anger You do not rebuke us, or chasten us in your wrath." (*Psalm 6:2*) Be sparing. It is enough for us if You deliver us from your great threat and from unknown and hidden torments. We dare not ask for complete forgiveness. How could we, when we have failed to keep our vow unstained, but after all Your past loving kindness and forgiveness have defiled it?

John Climacus, The Ladder of Divine Ascent

Reflection Questions

- What areas of self am I taking to task during this Great Fast?
- If not personally involved, how do I support my parish ECF Program?
- Do I try to set a good example for the youth of my parish?

THE FIFTH MONDAY OF THE GREAT FAST

Father Dr. Bryan R. Eyman

Behold, this is the time of grace and beauty; this glorious day is brilliant with fasting. Let us hasten, O faithful, to purify ourselves, that we may appear without stain before the Creator and share in his incomparable splendor, through the prayers of the all-holy Theotokos.

Matins Sessional Hymn II

Readings

Isaiah 37:33 – 38:6

Genesis 13:12-18

Proverbs 14:27 – 15:4

Meditation

"A time of grace and beauty?" A "glorious day ... brilliant with fasting?" How can this be? Why would be singing such a hymn in the midst of the Great Fast? Isn't the Great Fast to be a time of trial and grief? How can we sing of beauty, glory, and joy?

As I gaze into the face of our Lord on the icon of the Cross, I do not see terror. I see peace. I do not see the brutality of the crucifixion. I see the love of the God Who died to save the world. Through pain, suffering and death, we discover the glory and beauty of the Resurrection.

Grace? That Uncreated Energy of the Holy Trinity radiating through all eternity, restoring in all creation the beauty that God desired. The Divine Grace that perfects that which is imperfect, that transforms, indeed transfigures each of us to the depths of our very soul. The Energy that cleanses that soul, our whole being, indeed the whole world.

What does glory have to do with fasting? What does beauty have to do with fasting? Paradoxes, indeed. But they are the very paradoxes that God has chosen to draw us out of ourselves and draw us toward Him.

These are paradoxes, indeed visions, that we can only experience when we are centered on our Lord Jesus Christ, his Life, Death, Resurrection and Ascension. The challenge of seeing glory and beauty in fasting can only be faced in Christ. And in Christ we can enter into a relationship that transfigures us into really living human beings.

The secular world, the world in bondage to sin, cannot see the beauty and glory of fasting. They cannot see the beauty and glory in the lives of the repentant. They confuse beauty and glory with fame and wealth. They have exchanged the true worship of the Living God to the cult of personality. They call our freedom in Christ, bondage, and their bondage to sin, freedom.

The secular world cannot see the beauty of the life of the ascetic. They see fasting as a drudgery, and do not see the bondage of gluttony. They cannot understand the freedom of owning nothing, and never see their doors and locks as a cell containing their true gods.

The secular world runs hither and yon, and believes itself important by how busy it has become. But the person who enters into the quiet of God can discover what is truly important, and experience the beauty of becoming united to the Living God.

May this time of the Great Fast become a time of leaving "Time", or better yet, changing "Time" so that we can see the beauty, the glory, the brilliance, the peace of a God who loves, saves and transfigures his people into union with Him.

Reflection Questions

- Where do I see the beauty of God in the world around me?
- In the paradoxes of faith, how do I discover the love God has for me?
- How can I discover the freedom from material things, through the practices of the Great Fast?

THE FIFTH TUESDAY OF THE GREAT FAST

Msgr. William G. Levkulic

O search me, God, and know my heart. O test me and know my thoughts. See that I follow not the wrong path and lead me in the path of life eternal.

Psalm 139:23-24

Readings

Isaiah 40:18-31

Genesis 15:1-15

Proverbs 15:7-19

Meditation

We have already come a long way in our journey through the Great Fast; just a few more days and we will have reached a glorious and triumphant entry into the holy city in the company of our Lord Jesus Christ. With our limited vision we look back at the road we have traveled that seemed so difficult:

Why was it necessary to spend so much time in prayer and meditation? Why did we have to deny ourselves so many little pleasures of ordinary life? Did the fasting and self-denial accomplish anything other than making us a little lighter in weight?

The answers to these questions depend upon what goal we have in mind.

Yes, the joy of Flowery Sunday lies just ahead. All the difficulties of the Great Fast will pale in comparison to the triumphant welcome that Jesus will receive. The crowd of people will proclaim Him as the Messiah. His kingship will be declared. Was this the goal we had in mind?

Who can foresee that in just a few more days everything will be turned topsy-turvy? The newly acclaimed King will be branded as a criminal and put to death on a cross. This is certainly not the goal we had in mind during our journey.

Our brief journey through the Great Fast is much like our journey through life. We can live it only in the moment because we cannot know what will happen in the moments, the days, the months and years to come.

Our joy and satisfaction must consist in knowing that what we are doing now is the best that we can offer to God. Nothing less than our best is expected of us – nothing more than our best will be demanded of us.

Reflection Questions

- Am I setting my Lenten priorities to give the best portion of time I can for prayer and meditation?

- Aside from the fasting required during this holy penitential season, am I fasting from my favorite foods and activities – giving my best to this Fast?

- While we understand almsgiving to be primarily a monetary thing, have I considered almsgiving of my time in service to my Church and community?

THE FIFTH WEDNESDAY OF THE GREAT FAST

Sister Christopher Malcovsky, O.S.B.M.

Praising the most holy wood of the Cross; we adore your Supreme goodness, O Christ our God. By it you have crushed the power of the enemy; You have made it a sign for those who believe in You. In thanksgiving we also cry out: Grant that we may complete the time of the Fast in peace and joy.

Matins, Sessional Hymn II

Readings

Isaiah 41:4-14

Genesis 17:1-9

Proverbs 15:20 – 16:9

Meditation

I quiet myself, relax, close my eyes and picture myself before the Holy Cross. As I sit there in silence, I see before me Jesus carrying his Cross trough the streets of Jerusalem on the way to Calvary.

Jesus, who for the past three years has done so much good – healing the lame, curing the sick, giving sight to the blind – all of this seems to have been forgotten. We so easily forget all that the Lord does for us. We so quickly forget all of the good things that others do for us. How many blessings have I have received and forgotten?

Jesus also challenged many people – calling them to repent, to change their lives, to forget self and to think about others. He challenges me to repent, to change my life, to forget myself and to think about others.

I walk along with the crowd as they follow Jesus. I hear a group of people yelling at Jesus. I can't understand why they would yell at someone who has not hurt them. They are those who probably go along with the crowd, who do not ask, "why are they doing this – did He really do something wrong?"

How often I, too, go along with a group who criticizes what is being done. I don't take the time to find out the truth or to ask, "what has this person done that is wrong?"

Another group I see following close by Jesus wants to help Him. They are crying because they see an innocent Man suffer. They are pushed aside by the soldiers, but do not go away. They persevere and run to catch up to Jesus. They try to give Him a drink of water – they try to wipe the perspiration from his face.

I often think about helping others or visiting them – those who are elderly or sick. I, too, need to make the effort to do this. I can't put it aside or allow other things that come my way to make me change my mind.

As I gaze upon the Cross, I remember that Jesus died on it to save me. The Cross is a sign of our salvation. I will try to remember this when I make the sign of the Cross.

Reflection Questions

- Do I take time to remember how Jesus has helped me or even healed me?

- Do I take time now to thank Him for all He has done for me – for his suffering, for his dying on the Cross for me?

- If I haven't made any changes to better my life, can I do so before this Lenten Season comes to an end?

THE FIFTH THURSDAY OF THE GREAT FAST

Kathe Kress

I have brought you, O my soul, all the models of the Old Testament; imitate the deeds of the just friends of God and turn away from the example of the wicked.

I offer you the examples of the New Testament, calling you to compunction, O my soul. Be inspired by the just ones, turn away from sinners and stir up the grace of Christ, by fasting and prayer and the purity of your life.

Matins, Canon of St. Andrew of Crete, Odes 8 and 9

Readings

Isaiah 42:5-16

Genesis 18:20-33

Proverbs 16:17-33

Meditation

Today, at matins, we take the entire Canon of St. Andrew of Crete. The Church has wisely placed it so late in our Lenten journey as a wake up call "for the end is near." The Canon reminds us that the Bridegroom is coming and that we are the virgins, prepared and awake, lest we miss the Feast. The Canon takes us through the whole panorama of Salvation History, beginning with Adam, the patriarchs, prophets, kings, judges and heroes – both men and women – set forth as examples of friends of God.

We can see that these were historically real people who struggled with temptation, who sinned, yet humbled themselves in repentance to God. They sought forgiveness and the opportunity to make amends for their misdeeds. In faith, we believe this to be true and not myth. In faith, we take them as holy examples and guides for our own journey.

With Scripture before me, I scan through the men and women mentioned in the Canon of St. Andrew: Adam, Eve, Cain, Abel, Lamech, Seth, Enos, Enoch and Noah. I pause at the story of Sodom and Gomorrah, one of today's Old Testament readings. I contemplate sin's destructive effects and the mercy of my loving Father preserving the faithful remnant.

I marvel at the faithfulness of Abraham, our father in faith, who was willing to sacrifice his son in obedience to God. In the fullness of time, God held Himself in covenant with Abraham and his descendants, allowing his obedient Son to be sacrificed for us.

I see the results of Hagar's prideful boasting. I see Jacob's ladder and recall how the Church uses it to teach us the way of mystical ascent. I am warned not to sell my birthright to the Deceiver as did Esau. Job teaches me to submit to God.

The priest-king Melchizadek stands alone, a prefigurement of Christ; Habukuk points to Jesus' descent to unlock the gates of Hades to free the souls of the just. Joseph, too, foreshadows Christ in burial in the pit, and as a type of savior. Moses brought God's Law to the people, but through their disobedience, they prolonged their wanderings and arrival in the Promised Land.

All of the old points to Jesus, the New Adam. He is truly the Lover of mankind in his condescension to become the Incarnate Word. I can but prostrate myself, saying: "God be merciful to me, a sinner."

Reflection Questions

- How often do I turn to the Bible for study and reflection? Is it a regular part of my prayer life?

- Under the inspiration of the Holy Spirit, Scripture writers featured people who were saints or sinners, and oftentimes both. The difference between the two is shown to be repentance. Which specific Biblical figure's repentant spirit do I wish to imitate?

- Obedience is shown to be the mark of a saint. Jesus is exalted because He was "obedient unto death, even death on a cross". (*Philippians 2:8*) Obedience is particularly problematic in a modern independent and pluralistic society. How can I better incorporate the virtue of obedience in my life?

THE FIFTH FRIDAY OF THE GREAT FAST

Mary Ellen Dudick

Then God said, "Take your son, Isaac, your only one whom you love, and go to the land of Moriah. There you shall offer him up as a holocaust on a height I will point out to you."

Genesis 22:2

Readings

Isaiah 45:11-17

Genesis 22:1-18

Proverbs 17:17 – 18:5

Meditation

The Great Fast has always been a time for me to reflect on my faith as I prepare for the glorious Resurrection of Christ. As I was reflecting on the readings for the fifth Friday of the Great Fast, I focused on Genesis 22:1-18: "The Testing of Abraham". I believe that this period of meditation, prayer, fasting and giving is a good time for me to place myself in the hands of God – to trust God wholly and completely, just as Abraham did, as told in Genesis.

Abraham is asked by God to sacrifice his longed for son, his heir, Isaac, born to him and Sarah in their old age. God promised Abraham that through Isaac, all nations of the earth would find blessing. He would live to bear descendents of Abraham and Sarah, but God asks Abraham to sacrifice his son in a holocaust to prove his belief.

Scripture does not reveal the tortuous thoughts Abraham must have had when he was asked to sacrifice his son. With fire and knife, he led his son, who carried the wood for the holocaust, to the high place chosen by God.

I think of the parallel to Jesus' journey to the cross and his ultimate sacrifice for us. I try to imagine the powerful emotions that Abraham must have had leading Isaac to his death. I try to imitate this trust and devotion of both father and son and imagine the extreme relief when God's messenger tells Abraham not to proceed, that he should not lay a hand on the boy. God provides a ram caught in the thicket by the horn, and this becomes the sacrifice offered up by Abraham in place of his son.

As we come to the fifth week of the Great Fast, the promise of Resurrection is near. I think of Jesus who suffered for us, died for us and rose for us. I pray I can become the person I am trying to be – one who is journeying through this life to God. Abraham trusted that God would provide and truly believed his promise of heirs through Isaac. I pray I am able to place myself in the hands of God and to look for the signs that I am on the right path. I believe that reading this meditation book is a sign that I am being guided gently by God to change.

Reflection Questions

- As I look at my life, what is possible for me if I trust God?
- How can I learn to recognize the signs God may send me?
- How have I changed or grown as I take my journey of faith?

AKATHIST SATURDAY

Sister Agnes Knapik, O.S.B.

Hail, O you through whom joy will shine forth;
 hail, O you through whom the curse will disappear!
Hail, O Restoration of the fallen Adam;
 hail, O Redemption of the tears of Eve!
Hail, O Peak above the reach of human thought;
 hail, O Depth even beyond the sight of angels!
Hail, O you who have become a kingly throne;
 hail, O you who carries Him who carries all!
Hail, O Star who manifests the Sun;
 hail, O Womb of the divine incarnation!
Hail, O you through whom creation is renewed;
 hail, O you through whom the Creator becomes a babe!
Hail, O Bride and Maiden ever-pure!

Ikos I, Akathist Hymn

Readings

Hebrews 9:1-7, 24-28

Mark 8:27-31

Luke **10**:38-42 **11**:27-28

Meditation

I look at each phrase of the text. I quietly rest in each one. My heart and mind delight in the beautiful expressions of praise, which Gabriel addresses to Mary. I have forgotten how wonderful is Mary's role in our redemption.

These words are sublime poetry. And it is right to honor Mary with these greetings. But I will not forget the humanness of Mary, the joys she experienced and the struggles she endured as she accepted the consequences of her "yes" to God.

She was a strong woman who experienced much that is painful. Pregnant and unmarried, yet forgetful of self, she went to help her cousin Elizabeth. Chased by Herod, she became a refugee in Egypt, running to save her young child's life. She knew well what it is to have a son talked about, arrested, laughed at, executed.

Mary would not have understood what we so glowingly chant in these beautiful stanzas. And she did not know what her "yes" to God would entail. But she said "yes" anyway.

Today we concentrate on the positive. In the light of the knowledge of the Resurrection, we admire all the graces Mary has received from her Son. We look at her with love.

Mary is the hopeful woman, the faithful woman. She received the angel's greeting and responded in faith.

Can I be strong like she is? Can I believe in things I cannot see – to trust in God's providence? Can I resolve to live joyfully in difficult circumstances? Is it possible, because of God's outpouring love, that my life is equally life-giving as Mary's life?

Reflection Questions

- Can I make it a habit to ask Mary to take my prayers and works and present them to her Son? They would be more beautiful from having passed through her hands.

- Do I ask Mary to help me to be a strong person?

- Do I look beyond life's difficulties and live in joy and trust in God's providence as Mary did?

- Do I need to work at recognizing God's love in my life? Could I write a hymn about the many ways that God has graced me?

THE FIFTH SUNDAY OF THE GREAT FAST

Dennis M. Prestash, Deacon Candidate

Jesus said, "Simon, I have something to say to you." "Tell me, Teacher," he said. "Two people were in debt to a certain creditor; one owed five hundred days' wages and the other owed fifty. Since he forgave it for both, which of them will love Him more?" Simon said in reply, "The one, I suppose, whose larger debt was forgiven." He said to him, "you have judged rightly."

Luke 7:40-43

Readings

Galatians 3:23-29

Luke 7:36-50

Meditation

Today, we meditate on the person of Saint Mary of Egypt. In her, we see the greatness of the power of sin forgiven and the blessedness of humility restored.

Mary was a woman who fell from the grace of God and lived the life of a fallen woman. Hers is the story of passion converted and genuine love restored. Mary was a woman who sought pleasure in life for seventeen years until she took a fateful journey to Jerusalem for the Exaltation of the Precious and Life-Giving Cross.

Shamelessly and without repentance in her life, she tried to cross the threshold of the Church of the Holy Sepulchre with faithful Christians on their pilgrimage. However, Mary was prevented from entering the Church by some invisible force. At that moment, her sinfulness was revealed to her and the words of salvation gently touched the eyes of her heart.

Seeking the help of the Holy Theotokos with a solemn vow, she entered and saw the Life-Giving Cross. Mary beheld the greatness of the mystery of God and how the Lord accepted her repentance. She again prayed to the Theotokos. Mary then fulfilled her vow by crossing the River Jordan into the desert of repentance wherein forgiveness, humility, sorrow, and illumination became the holy elements of her life.

Mary's life of repentance highly exemplifies the Gospel of the Fifth Sunday of the Great Fast. A woman (Mary Magdalene) who had sinned grievously falls before the feet of our Lord. She weeps incessant tears, wipes those blessed feet with her hair and pours very expensive perfume on his feet. However, the Pharisees object to this precisely because she is a sinful woman. They see only the sin and not the person or the greatness of her love.

Icon of the sinful woman wiping the feet of Jesus (Luke 7:36-50)

Christ reveals that those who are forgiven much, love much. For Scripture states: "So I tell you, her many sins have been forgiven; hence, she has shown great love. But the one to whom little is forgiven, loves little." (*Luke 7:47*)

In today's Gospel, we have read that an unclean woman came to Christ who was clean, and she did not soil Him but, in fact, was made clean by Him. Can we expect less when we who are unclean come to that Lord to expect the same cleanliness?

Patristic Reading

The Initial stages of learning about religious devotion are naturally related to the flesh. For in our first encounter with religion we come into contact with the letter and not the spirit. But as we get nearer to the spirit and refine the materiality of words with the more subtle forms of contemplation, we come to dwell – as far as this is possible for man – purely in the pure Christ, so that we can say with Saint Paul, "Though we have known Christ according to the flesh, now we no longer know Him in this manner". (*2 Corinthians 5:16*) That is to say, we no longer know Him according to the flesh because, through the intellect's naked encounter with the Logos stripped of the veils covering Him, we have advanced from knowing Him according to the flesh to knowing his "glory as of the only begotten Son of the Father." (*John 1:14*)

He who is living the life in Christ has gone beyond the righteousness of both the Law and nature. This Saint Paul indicated when he said, "For in Christ Jesus there is neither circumcision nor uncircumcision." (*Galatians 5:6*) By circumcision he meant righteousness according to the Law; by uncircumcision he hinted at natural justice, or equity.

Some are reborn through water and the spirit; (*John 3:5*) others receive baptism in the Holy Spirit and in fire (*Matthew 3:11*). I take these four things – water, spirit, fire and Holy Spirit – to mean one and the same Spirit of God. To some the Holy Spirit is water because He cleanses the external stains of their bodies. To others He is simply spirit because He makes them active in the practice of virtue. To others He is fire because He cleanses the interior defilement which lies deep within their souls. To others according to Daniel, He is Holy Spirit because He bestows on them wisdom and spiritual knowledge (*Daniel 1:17; 5:11-12*). For the single identical Spirit takes his different names from the different ways in which He acts on each person.

Maximos the Confessor, Four Centuries on Theology

Reflection Questions

- Have I ever meditated on the mercy of God?

- Have I realized my uncleanness before God or am I afraid to soil Him?

- How great is my love and/or forgiveness in today's society?

THE SIXTH MONDAY OF THE GREAT FAST

Sister Margaret Mary Schima, O.S.B.

Listen to me, all of you in far-off lands. The Lord called me before by birth. From within the womb He called me by my name. God will make my words of judgment sharp as swords. He has hidden me in the shadow of his hand. I am like a sharp arrow in his quiver.

He said to me, "You are my Servant, a Prince of Power with God, and you shall bring me glory."

I replied, "But my work for them seems all in vain. I have spent my strength for them without response. Yet I leave it all with God for my reward."

Isaiah 49:1-4

Readings

Isaiah 48:17 – 49:4

Genesis 27:1-41

Proverbs 19:16-25

Meditation

The same reference from the Book of Isaiah is used in the prayers for the feast of John the Baptist. God has his particular designs for each person. He plans his designs before each one is born. Because of free will, given by God, it is up to each person to carry out God's plan.

Humans do not always do in their lives what God calls them to do. Just as John the Baptist was chosen to prepare the people of Israel for Jesus coming on this earth, so God calls each person to fulfill a task for which He planned.

This week the Church reminds us of the great task God asked of Jesus – the redeeming of mankind through his death on the cross. All are reminded of the events of the last weeks and days before the death of Jesus.

Reflection Questions

- What has God planned for me in my life?

- Have I fulfilled his call? Or have I given some excuse, or just said, "no"?

- What can I learn from John the Baptist, who was called before he was born?

- What can I learn from Jesus, Who was called before He was born?

Icon of Christ taken down from the Cross

THE SIXTH TUESDAY OF THE GREAT FAST

Father Jack Custer

I have kept you and given you as a covenant to the people, to establish the land, to apportion the desolate heritages; saying to the prisoners, "Come forth," and to those in darkness, "appear."

Isaiah 49:8-9 (RSV)

Readings

Isaiah 49:6-10

Genesis 31:3-16

Proverbs 21:3-21

Meditation

God addresses these words through the prophet to His "Servant", whose career mysteriously foreshadows the Passion and Resurrection of our Lord. The Suffering Servant of Isaiah's prophecies offered comfort and the promise of new life to a generation driven into exile and despair by its own unfaithfulness to their covenant promise to be God's people. The Servant's rejection and humiliation by his own people, his suffering and even his death, became a means of making many people righteous before God again (*Isaiah 53:11*).

Our hymnography (*Sticheron at Psalm 140, Tone 5, Saturday*) imagines Jesus Himself crying "Come forth" to the dead imprisoned in Hades, pathetic, helpless, and unable to win heaven on their own merits. We too can only hope to be invited into the Heavenly Banquet; we can only accept our place in the Heavenly Bridal Chamber as a gift unearned.

Our Lenten Journey has Resurrection as its goal. We look forward to the Resurrection on the last day and we struggle to overcome whatever sinfulness would prevent us from being with our Lord forever. We also have the opportunity to enjoy a gift of new life even now, when we celebrate the Pascha of Christ's Resurrection liturgically this year. We can only rise with Christ, however, if we dare to identify and reject the power of sin and death in our lives.

Our Lord said at the Last Supper: "This is eternal life, to know You, the one true God and Him whom You have sent, Jesus Christ." (*John 17:3*) Death reigns whenever we choose not to know Christ in our neighbor (*Matthew 25:30*). We experience Death whenever we prefer the darkness of unchallenged faults, unquestioned habits, unexamined attitudes of judgmentalism or pride.

Today's matins hymns challenge us to see our prison in the attitude of indifference: "Bound by the chains of sin, O my soul, you have fallen into laziness and inaction". (*Matins Aposticha*)

Tonight, at vespers, the death of Lazarus challenges us to see the power of death in our own lives. We are "worn out by the disease of sin and lying on the bed of despair;" (*Matins Sidalen*) our soul "lies in the tomb of laziness, hardened as the rock of the tomb." (*Vespers Sticheron*)

We know that on Saturday Lazarus will be called forth from his tomb. Wherever we are imprisoned and deprived of the fullness of life by sin, we can reach out for the life-giving hand of our Lord and hear Him say to us: "Come forth!"

Reflection Questions

- Do I see myself in a covenant relationship with my God? Can I name the ways in which He has been faithful to me? Have I discerned clearly how He wants me to be faithful in return?

- Where is my heritage, my spiritual life, "desolate"? Where do I experience lifelessness and barrenness in my own life? How have my own choices contributed to these experiences?

- Do my habits, attitudes, or actions bind me or imprison me? Do I imprison others by co-opting them in my own sins or by refusing them forgiveness or the freedom to grow and change?

THE SIXTH WEDNESDAY OF THE GREAT FAST

Father Joseph Bertha, Ph.D. Candidate

As the children of old, let us go out to meet Christ our God; in place of palms, let us offer the mercy of our hearts; in prayer, let us wave our branches, crying: Hosanna!

Matins Canon, Ode 8

Readings

Isaiah 58:1-11

Genesis 43:26 – 45:16

Proverbs 21:23 – 22:4

Meditation

Mercy is a great gift that God gives so graciously and freely to all of us. Our Divine Liturgy of St. John Chrysostom is replete with appeals to God's mercy. For instance, we chant the petition invoking God the Father in the Incessant Litany "O Lord almighty, God of our fathers, we pray you, hear and have mercy".

Jesus Christ, who is the icon of God the Father, reflects this abundant mercy in his life. We only need to look at how iconographers represent this everlasting mercy in the manner that our Lord's eyes are portrayed in the icon. Choose for your meditation any icon of Jesus Christ and take careful notice of his gaze.

The iconographer represents the eyes of our Lord in a special way, and not as we normally expect as human beings. Notice that his right eye looks directly at the viewer, while the left eye of our Lord looks off to the distance. This is an intentional arrangement used by iconographers to indicate the compassionate mercy of Jesus Christ.

The right eye is the view of justice and the law. This is the look of a judge confronting the accused with a stern head-on gaze. We sinners ask ourselves the question posed by this eye, "You did what?" On the other side, the left eye denotes compassion, by looking away. This reminds me of the compassionate look of the Prodigal Son's father, who does not confront his son with justice, but he looks into the distance, the direction of compassion, where he indeed recognizes his son from afar.

This is the very same wonderful look of mercy that God the Father regards us through his Icon and Son, Jesus Christ. We sinners need to recognize, develop and practice looking at each other with that same gaze, for we too are created in the icon and likeness of God.

Throughout our lifetime, we have many opportunities to live the life of mercy, by asking God for his boundless mercy in the Sacrament of Penance and Reconciliation. We are fortunate to have the refulgent icons of our Lord and Savior Jesus Christ to be able to gauge our progress and to serve as a reminder of the path of holiness we need to follow in order to become living icons of the Father's mercy!

Reflection Questions

- Inasmuch as I have benefited from God's merciful eye, is there someone who has injured me or my family, to whom I need to turn my merciful eye? I will pray for the grace to follow our Lord's example.

- When did I last take the time to gaze upon an icon of our Lord and become the beloved object of his mercy? I need to set aside time during the remainder of the Lenten season to do just that.

THE SIXTH THURSDAY OF THE GREAT FAST

Sister Margaret Ann Andrako, O.S.B.M.

Let us yoke together both action and contemplation and send them as ambassadors to Christ, that by his coming, He may give life to our spirit which is as lifeless as Lazarus in the tomb. Let us offer to Him our palms of righteousness and cry out: Blessed is He who comes in the name of the Lord.

Matins, Sessional Hymn II

Readings

Isaiah 65:8-16

Genesis 46:1-7

Proverbs 23:15 – 24:5

Meditation

We've all seen the picture: a farmer in the 19th century tilling the land with his oxen, and we notice the heavy yoke that harnesses the oxen together to steady their path as they are led in the plowing field.

Now, let us fast forward to this day and age – this time and place – nearing the end of the Great Fast. Today the liturgical hymns of our Church urge us to "yoke together" action and contemplation. At an initial reading, we may be inclined to think that these qualities are on opposite ends of the spectrum. With a closer look and some reflection, we realize that they are not mutually exclusive, but rather complementary forces in our lives.

Each year when we set out upon the Great Fast, we are reminded by our Church that prayer, fasting and almsgiving is the tripod meant to support and sustain us during our journey. We are encouraged during these days to be more focused in practicing good works and in spending more time in prayer. We are called to action and contemplation!

I am sure that not one of us would deny the "action" in our lives, but I believe we need to look at this action to decide if it is worthy of God or just frenetic energy. Sometimes we can get caught up in the busyness of life – doing things without much thought. But we are much more than what we do. For our spiritual lives to be developing, we need to consider who we are and how we relate to God. In order for this to occur we need quiet time – some time each day for prayer and reflection.

Prayer is our personal response to God's presence in our lives. In our personal prayer, we approach God with a listening heart to respond to God's love so we, in turn, can share this love with others. Our relationship with God prompts us to action – to be a sign of hope for others, to bring his healing presence to a hurting broken world that is so yearning for wholeness. This "action" takes many forms. It is all the ordinary events that make up our daily life: working to earn a living; caring for spouse and children, or elderly or ill family members; attending school; visiting parishioners in the hospital or assisted living places; offering hospitality to guests; volunteering in a soup kitchen; the list goes on, as diverse as the number of people reading these words.

What we do is not as important as how we do it. If we invite God into our lives, into all these seemingly insignificant details, we become conscious that we do them with God, and our action and contemplation are integrated. Far from being polar opposites, they are now truly yoked together – they are our ambassadors to Christ. When I go about my day, doing my ordinary actions with God, I realize that it is God who enables me to share his love and makes me realize how much I need him. My actions draw me back to God in prayer – in contemplation – where I can thank Him for allowing me to be his instrument; where I can plumb the depths of my spirit to see where God may be calling me to act next. Let us, then, be mindful of the interplay of action and contemplation in our lives, in and out of the season of the Great Fast!

Reflection Questions

- When and where will I find time for contemplation in my life?

- How attentive am I in my quiet time to discover the actions that God calls me to do?

- Do the actions I perform send me back to the Lord to reflect how I have brought Him to others?

- Do I remember to thank God for the good He inspires me to do?

THE SIXTH FRIDAY OF THE GREAT FAST

Sister Marion Dobos, O.S.B.

The prophets have revealed you through symbols, as the gate, the mountain and the holy tabernacle, the bright cloud from whom the Sun of justice and our only Light has risen, for those seated in darkness and gloom.

Matins, Ode 8

Readings

Isaiah 66:10-24

Genesis 49:33 – 50:26

Proverbs 31:8-31

Meditation

The literature of the early church resounds with praise of holy women and the calendar of the church is full of female saints whose prestige is of equal worth to that of the greatest male saints. The attendance of the women disciples upon Jesus, most especially their presence at his trial and crucifixion, their preparation for his burial and their journey to the tomb on the third day, remind us all of the divine mission women played in the life of Jesus.

This beautiful quote from Matins describes Mary, Theotokos, and model for all humanity. The stories of biblical women have unique characteristics in showing us what it means to be a woman created in the image of God. The Old Testament passage from Proverbs prescribed for today tells us about the qualities and virtues of "The Capable Wife". In this Old Testament reading we see Mary being prefigured and one of the many ways the Holy Spirit prepared us for her mission here on earth.

Mary gave a full human nature to the Second Person of the Holy Trinity. Her personality penetrates the mind and heart of the believer, not only because she is the Mother of God, but also as a person who handled such a divine mission with grace, commitment and fulfillment. She is the prototype of all we are to be. In this woman we see a model of faith, an example of what God has in store for all who say "yes" to his loving call.

Reflection Questions

- With what qualities of Mary's personality do I most identify?

- In what ways am I growing in the knowledge and appreciation of what my divine mission is in life?

- During this time of the Great Fast, in what ways have I responded to God's call?

LAZARUS SATURDAY

Mary G. P. Rhoads

O Lord, When You said to Martha: "I am the Resurrection," You confirmed Your words by actions, calling Lazarus from Hades. Through my passions I am dead; raise me also, I beseech You, in Your tender love for mankind.

Matins, At the Praises, Tone 8

Readings

Hebrews 12:28 – 13:8

John 11:1-45

Meditation

"Through my passions I am dead ..."
Through my passion for food I am dead
     to the hungry.
Through my passion for money I am dead
     to the poor and needy.
Through my passion for power I am dead
     to the powerless.
Through my passion for sex I am dead
     to the innocent and pure of heart.
Through my passion for [*insert sin*] I am dead
     to [*insert sin's effect*].
Through my passions I am dead
     to all the good I can do for God's Kingdom.

During the Great Fast we strive to be better people by our fasting, praying and almsgiving. We have set aside our passions and have prayed more for our families, our church, our community and ourselves. These actions free us to focus on the good we can do for God's Kingdom.

When Jesus called Lazarus from the tomb, Lazarus rose up – he listened to Christ's words and obeyed them. Then Jesus said: "Untie him". And they untied Lazarus making him free to see Christ again and be in his presence.

Just as Jesus' actions brought life and freedom to Lazarus, our actions of fasting and charity will also lead us to God's life and freedom.

Let this be our prayer:

As Lazarus heard You from the tomb, let me hear You call my name from the tomb of my sins and passions, O Lord. As Lazarus was untied from the cloth, let me also be untied from the hold of my passions that prevent me from seeing the hungry, poor, powerless and innocent. For only then can I truly be in your presence and work for your Kingdom. Amen.

As we come to the end of our Lenten Journey, let us be untied from our passions so that we may see Christ and be in his presence and feel Him and touch Him in all the people and circumstances He puts in our life, so that rather than serving our desires and passions, we will serve Him and his Kingdom.

Reflection Questions

- Where has my focus been during this Holy Season? Have I been building my kingdom or the Lord's?

- Do I understand that this is what we pray when we say "Thy kingdom come" in the Lord's Prayer?

- Which passions have I been cooperating with the Lord to unbind from me?

FLOWERY (Palm) SUNDAY

Father James Spontak

Let us all gather this day, the new Israel, the church of the Gentiles, and with the prophet Zechariah, let us say: "Rejoice, O daughter Zion, shout for joy, O daughter Jerusalem; behold, your King comes to you; He is the Savior, meek and humble, seated on the foal of a donkey, a beast of burden." Carrying palms, let us praise Him as did the children: Hosanna in the highest; blessed is He who is coming, the King of Israel.

Vespers, Stichera at Psalm 140

Readings

Philippians 4:4-9

John 12:1-18

Meditation

Today, Palm (Flowery) Sunday strikes a unique chord in the range of our spiritual and emotional dispositions: "Rejoice heartily, O daughter Zion, shout for joy, O daughter Jerusalem." (*Zechariah 9:9*)

The Church observes this as a festal day of joy, for it is the arrival of the King, a savior who establishes justice and restores his people. In the lesson from Philippians, the same mood is reiterated and emphasized: "Rejoice in the Lord always, again I will say, Rejoice ... The Lord is near." (*Philippians 4:4-5*)

Yet this is a moment with even more specific detail in its timbre and tone. The joy in welcoming the Lord to Jerusalem recognizes the scope of all that will occur there in only a few days. In the Gospel, hushed rumors of the awaiting drama intrude into our awareness.

The chief priests are indignant at the joyful "Hosannas" of the Hebrew children (*Matthew 21:15*). Their indignation sows seeds of plots to murder Lazarus (*John 12:10*) as well as Jesus. The greed of Judas (*John 12:4-6*) will yield eventual betrayal. And where the echoes of "Hosanna" linger in Jerusalem streets, there will soon be the coarse and angry shouts of "Crucify Him."

The joy of Palm Sunday appears to be shaken, even shattered, by the lengthening shadow that casts itself over the next several days. The unfolding story of Great and Holy Week brings betrayal, public rejection and crucifixion. But our joy perdures, it lasts, it conquers. This joy is rooted in something much deeper. Its source is the Paschal Mystery, which is now being renewed among us.

The kontakion of today's feast reminds us that "We have been buried with you through Baptism, O Christ our God, and we have become worthy of immortal life by your Resurrection." Here is the pattern of our Christian existence, the rhythm of the ongoing and unfolding process of transformation that began at our Baptism.

Icon of the Entry into Jerusalem

It is this, which allows us to face, and to wrestle with the disillusionment, the disappointment, the bewilderment that are part of the life of a Christian. All of these are somehow portrayed and reflected through the events of Holy Week. When we engage in this struggle, faith matures, joy is renewed, "and the peace of God which surpasses all understanding will keep your minds and your hearts in Christ Jesus." (*Philippians 4:7*)

Patristic Reading

"Much people of the Jews therefore knew that He was there, and they came, not for Jesus' sake only, but that they might see Lazarus also, who He had raised from the dead."

As wealth is wont to hurl into destruction those who are not heedful, so also is power; the first leads into covetousness, the second into pride. See, for instance, how the subject multitude of the Jews is sound, and their rulers corrupt; for that the first of these believed Christ, the Evangelists continually assert, saying, that "many of the multitude believed on Him;" (*John 7:31, 48*) but they who were of the rulers, believed not. And they themselves say, not the multitude, "Hath any of the rulers believed on Him?" But what saith one? "The multitude who know not God are accursed;" (*John 7:49*) the believers they call accursed, and themselves the slayers, wise. In this place also, having beheld the miracle, the many believed; but the rulers were not contented with their own evil deeds, they also attempted to kill Lazarus.

Suppose they did attempt to slay Christ because He broke the Sabbath, because He made Himself equal to the Father, and because the Romans whom ye allege, yet what charge had they against Lazarus, that they sought to kill him? Is having received a benefit a crime? Seest thou how murderous is their will? Yet He had worked many miracles; but none exasperated them so much as this one, not the paralytic, not the blind. For this was more wonderful in its nature, and was wrought after many others and it was a strange thing to see one, who had been dead four days, walking and speaking. To them it would be an honorable action, in truth, to mix up the solemn assembly for the feast with murders. So that they would have done the same in the case of the blind man, had it not been in their power to find fault respecting the Sabbath. Besides, the man was of no one, and they cast him out of the temple;

but Lazarus was a person of distinction, as is clear, since many came to comfort his sisters; and the miracle was done in the sight of all, and most marvelously. On which account all ran to see.

This then stung them, that while the feast was going on, all should leave it and go to Bethany. They set their hand therefore to kill Him, and thought they were not daring anything, so murderous were they. On this account the Law at its commencement opens with this, "Thou shalt not kill;" (*Exodus 20:13*) and the Prophet brings this charge against them, "Their hands are full of blood." (*Isaiah 1:15*)

John Chrysostom, Homily LXVI

Reflection Questions

- Do I allow the mood, the atmosphere prescribed by the seasons of the Church – particularly the Great Fast and this present time of Holy Week – to influence my life, my home, my family? Is the spirit or environment of my own circumstances in harmony with this season or in constant tension with it?

- Is joy a pervasive and consistent disposition of my Christian life, one that endures and is manifest even when I may face disillusionment or disappointment?

- How am I called to mature in my faith during Holy Week this year? In particular, how can I identify more fully with the Paschal Mystery – of having been buried with Christ through Baptism so that I might come to new life through his Resurrection?

HOLY MONDAY

Msgr. Russell Duker, SEOD

This present day ushers in with splendor the Passion of the Lord ...
the Creator draws near ...
enduring all things to secure salvation for humanity.

Bridegroom Matins, Third Sessional Hymn

Readings

Ezekiel 1:1-20	Job 1:1-12
Exodus 1:1-20	Matthew 24:3-35

Meditation

A renowned American archeologist led an expedition to the Nile Valley. He hired an aged Egyptian man to serve as his guide and to navigate his small craft through the treacherous rapids of the precarious Nile River.

As these two men began their journey, the professor condescendingly began to question the old man: "Do you know the history of your country and of the pharaohs? Do you understand the ancient hieroglyphic script? Did you ever learn to read and write?"

Somewhat embarrassed, the elderly Egyptian guide replied negatively to each of the questions. And as he was making his apologies, the boat suddenly capsized.

In the ensuing confusion, the boatman yelled to the professor, "Do you know how to swim?"

"No!" came the emphatic reply. He knew so much, except the one thing that really counted in this situation. Because of his ignorance regarding this one small thing, the erudite Egyptologist perished.

We now stand at the threshold of Passion Week, the most solemn week of the year, and the most important thing for us to realize is that our salvation is at hand. Yesterday's holy epistle lesson at the Divine Liturgy for Flowery Sunday set the theme for Passion Week. The Holy Apostle Paul tells us: "Rejoice in the Lord always! The Lord is *near!*" (*Philippians 4:4-5*) "The hour has come, and it is time for everything to be accomplished [our salvation]." (*John 12:23*)

The Lord is ***near,*** and He has come to secure redemption for the entire human race. This is the most important thing that we must know. Indeed it is the only thing that really counts.

On Holy Monday, the Church presents Christ to us as the "Bridegroom". Jesus comes to redeem his bride – the Church. And who is this Church but the people of God – us? The Bridegroom Jesus thus comes to secure salvation for us – his bride – and to bring us into his bridal chamber – the "New Jerusalem", the "Holy Zion", the "New Life" with Him in eternity.

The beautiful and eloquent services of Passion Week help us to deepen our spiritual insight. It is through our participation in the liturgical worship services that we most concretely can demonstrate our love for Jesus and the redemptive acts that He now goes to perform in our behalf.

Reflection Questions

- Awakened by the Church's call that the Bridegroom is near, how have we prepared for his arrival?

- What lessons have we gleaned from the Great Fast services and readings that pointed to our salvation won by Christ through his sacrifice?

- Have we swept our spirit of the leaven of sin to prepare for Pascha by making time for the Mystery of Reconciliation?

HOLY TUESDAY

Father Thomas Wesdock

O faithful, let us be on fire with love for the Bridegroom, and with lamps burning, let us go to meet Him. May the light of our virtues shine brightly, and may our faith be radiant.

Matins, First Sessional Hymn, Tone 4

Readings

Ezekiel 1:21-28	Job 1:13-22
Exodus 2:5-10	Matthew 24:36 – 26:2

Meditation

Holy Week, for me, is the highlight of the Journey through the Great Fast. What we, as a Church, have been anticipating for so long during time of the Great Fast, is now very near. The remembrance of the death and Resurrection of our Lord and Savior Jesus Christ is lived out once again in the Liturgy of our Church.

After a long and oftentimes difficult struggle through the six weeks of the Great Fast, the first three days of Holy Week, with their Bridegroom Matins in the morning and their Presanctified liturgies in the evening, are an oasis of refreshment, a change of pace from the Great Fast schedule. These days prepare us with their focus on Christ the Bridegroom, to enter into this most sacred time of the entire Church year – the time when Christ reveals the immensity of his great love for us. His love for us is that of a Bridegroom for his dearly beloved, which not even the bonds of death can destroy.

These days of spiritual refreshment, the first three days of Holy Week, are marked by their continuously lengthening days of early spring. They serve as a sign to everyone of what is to come in the near future, both physically in nature and metaphorically in the Liturgy of our Church. They reveal to us that the long dark days of winter are passing very rapidly and that the sun is ready to rise again into the blue spring sky from behind the dark gray clouds in which it has been entombed most of the winter.

Once again, the sun's rays are ready to shine forth upon the earth, bringing warmth and brightness to a world overshadowed at times by what can seem like great darkness. The sun gives us hope that there are better days ahead. The warmth and brightness of the sun can be seen as a symbol of the hope that Christ's Resurrection brings to the world, the hope in a better future, in a world fully enlightened by God's love and peace.

And that is where our attention is drawn during these first three days of Holy Week, to the true Son Who gives us that hope, the Son Who would give Himself up to the darkness of the Cross out of love for us. He is the Bridegroom Whom we seek, the One Who would give up everything for his beloved, and He truly has done that for each and every one of us.

This week's events will immerse us in the revelation of God's infinite and unfailing love for us if we allow ourselves to be drawn the Christ through the liturgical celebrations of this Holy Week.

Then, we truly will be able to enter the bridal chamber of God with Christ, which is the tomb at Golgotha, to emerge as one with Christ, victorious in his Holy Resurrection. Each will become a new person with Christ, experiencing the fruits of his Holy Resurrection – peace and joy – even now, in our lives.

Behold, the Bridegroom is near! Let us purify ourselves in these last remaining days of Holy Week, that our lamps may be shining brightly for the Lord when He comes. Now is the time to make ourselves ready, to be filled with the love of Christ, Who gives Himself to us again this Holy Week, and each and every day we allow his true light to shine in our hearts.

Reflection Questions

- Do I plan to take advantage of the opportunity to refresh myself with the Bread of Life given at the Presanctified liturgies offered by the Church during the first three days of Holy Week?

- Have I prepared to welcome the Bridegroom by cleaning my spiritual house and going to confession?

HOLY WEDNESDAY

Deacon Nicholas A. Daddona

... behold me sunk in sin, filled with despair by reason of my deeds, yet not rejected by Thy love.

Aposticha

Readings

Ezekiel 2:3 – 3:3   Job 2:1-10

Exodus 2:11-22   Matthew 26:6-16

Meditation

It is interesting to note that this verse gives us a picture of what it means to be loved by God.

Unfortunately, it is not so uncommon for people to transgress the laws of God. It is easy to fall into sin. Most people realize that this is part of the human situation. Once this does happen, the question remains how do we approach our loving God to help us deal with our sin and despair? How does one face God after one has violated his laws? How do we feel when it gets to be too much and our sinfulness brings us to a time of despondency?

Just as a loving child needs the support of his/her parents when something is wrong, so does the person who has sinned need the loving support of God. How many of us believe that this support is there for us? The Aposticha verse tells us though we have sunk into despair, God will not reject us. Even though our deeds may pull us down, his love is there to lift us up.

This concept must be understood by us in order to fully understand God's mercy. His love for us will be the hand that brings us to Him and the pat on the shoulder that gives us the courage to move on. No matter how horrible the deed or how deep we fall, his love will never reject us.

Today we come to Church and the mercy of God is extended to us in the Sacrament of Holy Anointing. Here is where we feel God's embrace. His love is offered to us to heal and strengthen us – never to destroy or to reject us.

As we enter the last days of Holy and Great Week, we should realize how much Our Lord's mercy is prevalent. Let us remember this fact and always rely on it. No matter how far we stray or transgress, the Father's love will never reject us, but will embrace and transform us.

Reflection Questions

- In my most sinful, darkest hours, have I remembered to fall at the feet of Jesus and seek his mercy? When I have done this, has He not always generously forgiven and comforted my despairing soul?

- Have I, in turn, sought to generously forgive others, even when they fail to seek my forgiveness?

- As I draw closer to remembering the day of sublime mercy when Jesus died for us even though we were still in sin, have I forgiven those who have wronged me and sought forgiveness of those I have wronged?

HOLY THURSDAY

Father David M. Petras, SEOD

Come, O faithful, let us raise our minds on high and enjoy the Master's hospitality and the table of immortal life in the upper room; and let us hear the exalted teaching of the Word whom we magnify.

Matins Ikos, Ode 9

Readings

Exodus 19:10-19

Job **38**:1-21 **42**:1-5

Isaiah 50:4-11

1 Corinthians 11:23-32

Matthew 26:2-20

John 13:3-17

Matthew 26:21-39

Luke 22:43-45

Matthew 26:40 – 27:2
(*taken as one Gospel*)

Meditation

In Holy Week the Passover mystery of the death and Resurrection of our Lord is represented in a much more vivid way than the rest of the year. The salvation accomplished then in history by Jesus, the Son of God and Messiah, is always present for our life, but when we commemorate it in the Holy and Great Week, it renews its pattern in the way we believe and live. The week begins in victory, Jesus enters the city as the King of Israel, and is welcomed by the people in a triumphal procession. However, in the middle of the week, He is betrayed by one of his disciples, as the Alleluia verse announces, "Thus even my friend, in whom I trusted, who ate my bread, has turned against me." (*Psalm 40:10*)

The mystery begins with hope. Our Lord explains what He is about to do, and He makes it eternal by establishing the sacramental mystery of Holy Communion. Today begins the mystery, and our Lord tells us it will destroy our sins and bring us eternal life. The Divine Liturgy we celebrate today makes real for us the presence of the Son of God, whose love is present for us now as truly as the first Holy Thursday.

Today we are invited to a double banquet, united in the one person, Jesus Christ our Lord. It is a banquet of words, for He tells us today of God's transcendent love for us in giving Himself entirely to us. "Today we have heard his sweet words, 'This is my Body which is broken for you and given for the forgiveness of sins'." (*Ambon Prayer*) Today He accomplishes his words by giving us his Body and Blood in the form of bread and wine. Only He can do this because Jesus is the incarnate Word of God.

Reflection Questions

- Do we come to the Passover mystery with the humility to accept the gift that is offered today – a gift beyond our power to comprehend?

- Is God's love the greatest reality in our lives? Do we love God with our whole heart and mind and soul and our neighbor as ourselves?

- How will our faith that we truly receive the Body and Blood of the Lord in Holy Communion change us?

Icon of Jesus Christ Washing the Feet of the Disciples

GREAT AND HOLY FRIDAY

Frederick M. Petro

O, how could the lawless council condemn to death the King of Creation without being ashamed at the thought of his good works which He recounted to them saying: "O my people, what have I done to you? Have I not filled Judea with miracles? Have I not raised the dead with a word? Have I not cured infirmities and sufferings? So now, what do you give to me in return? Why have you not remembered me? For the healing you have wounded me; for life you give me death; you hang me, your benefactor, on a tree as a criminal. You treat me, the Lawgiver, as a lawbreaker. You condemn the King of all." O long suffering Lord, glory be to You.

Vespers Hymn

Readings

Exodus 33:11-23	Matthew 27:1-38
Job 42:12-17	Luke 23:39-43
Isaiah 52:13 – 54:1	Matthew 27:39-54
1 Corinthians 1:18 – 2:2	John 19:31-37
	Matthew 27:55-61
	(taken as one Gospel)

Meditation

Recollections of Great and Holy Friday ... for some reason the sky always seemed gray – you didn't turn on the television or radio – even children wanted to keep the strict fast – and most stores were closed from noon to three. You did two things that day – go to church, or get ready to go to church. Obviously, that was some time back, so how do we meditate now, on the most solemn day of the liturgical calendar?

For the benefit of those not from the Eastern Christian tradition, or with limited experience, we can note that the services of the day are one continuous meditation. Plan to attend the matins service with 12 distinct Gospel readings, and/or the Burial Vespers (evening service).

The passion narrative is replete with images for thought. After the fourth matins Gospel, we sing: "O Lord, when you willingly came to the time of your passion, You cried out to your disciples: 'If you cannot keep watch with Me for just one hour, why did you promise that you would even die for Me?' ..."

Let's travel through time to that first Great and Holy Friday. We can identify with his disciples, not staying alert spiritually in prayer, or in real life situations by not attending to those around us who are in need. We may not be sleeping, but our e-mails, voice mails, call waiting and other distractions are pulling us away from prayer and prayerful activity.

The disciples were not alone. "Joseph, with Nicodemus, took You down from the cross, your body clothed in glory as with a robe; but seeing You lifeless, naked and unburied, began to weep and lament ..." (*Vespers Aposticha*) There were others, too – Simon of Cyrene, the myrrh-bearing women and the unnamed bystanders – all speechless because their leader, their Savior, was swallowed by death.

With them we wonder how He Who performed miracles, raised Lazarus and cured the sick is now treated as a criminal and condemned to death. (*Vespers, Hymn 6*)

God's plan is a mystery. As we grow in maturity, our understanding of this plan is no clearer now than when we were children. Our only understanding is through faith, faith in Jesus Christ, today in the tomb, but only fully understood as our Risen Lord.

Reflection Questions

- Are we standing with the Arimathean and other followers, or are we meandering about with the unrepentant thief and the mindless soldiers who could think only of throwing dice for Jesus' garments?

- How have I grown in understanding through prayer, fasting and almsgiving this Great Lent?

GREAT SATURDAY

Father Robert J. Karl

"All you who have been baptized into Christ have put on Christ, Alleluia!"

Galatians 3:27

Readings

Ezekiel 37:1-14	Jonah 1:1 – 4:11
1 Corinthians 5:6-8	Joshua 5:10-15
Galatians 3:13-14	Exodus 13:20 – 15:19
Matthew 27:62-66	Daniel 3:1-90
Genesis 1:1-13	Romans 6:3-11
Exodus 12:1-11	Matthew 28:1-20

Meditation

The Great Fast prepares us to go with Christ into Jerusalem and his passion, crucifixion and death and to his glorious Resurrection. There is something about the Cross, passion and death of Christ that grasps our attention and many even find it appealing. We become captivated by the Cross upon which hung the Savior of the world. At times a greater part of our observance centers therein and we remain steadfast at the tomb. In the meantime, the world weaves a new focus for Easter – egg hunts, bunnies, Easter fashions, kolbasi and pretty Easter eggs – all given more attention than the glorious Resurrection.

Then the silence and the darkness, the fasting and prayer of Holy Saturday envelops us. We read from the Old Testament stories of "the beginning" and how "it was good" and then we hear Paul's question: "Are you not aware that we who were baptized in Christ Jesus were baptized into his death? ... through baptism into his death we were buried with Him, so that just as Christ was raised from the dead by the Glory of the Father, we too might live a new life. ..." (*Romans 6:3-11*)

Remember, Christ said "For this hour have I come", (*John 12:27*) that the Son of God enters death – the duel between Christ and death – Christ and Satan. Christ as God-Man – the Source of Life – the Son of God, dies – and God Himself enters the realm of death and partakes of death, and from within – God overcame and destroyed death and by death He conquered death.

We must come to see our world and ourselves in the light of God's grace. In Christ our lives are transformed and we must accept it – choose it – and it will permeate our lives with blazing light of the glorious Resurrection. This same Christ calls us to renew and face struggle and change of heart within each of us – the struggle we were pledged into at our baptism.

We can live the true joy of the good news with all its truth and transforming power – the struggle of putting off the old and putting on the new. We prayerfully discover more deeply each year that the way we have chosen is set against so much of the world. We must clear our sights, renew our baptism into Christ and undergo our own Passover from sin to freedom, from darkness to light and from death to life – only then do we dare to act as if God has reordered our life here and now.

The emerging shapes of our lives in Christ happens again every year. And then, in our transformation in Christ, we can burst forth from our tombs and celebrate our new lives in the Resurrected Christ – a new people, full of joy and hope and confidence!

This day, Great Saturday, with its quiet space and deep silence, belongs to us. In our silence, prayer and fasting, it gives us the opportunity to renew and transform our lives. Then with uplifted hearts we may joyfully sing the paschal hymn:

"This is the Resurrection, O people, let us be enlightened by it. The Passover is the Lord's Passover. He has brought us from death to life ... yesterday I was buried with You O Lord, but today I rise resurrected with You. Yesterday I crucified my self with You O Savior, now glorify me in your Kingdom." (*Matins Canon, Odes 1 and 3*)

Reflection Questions

- Am I not aware that we who were baptized in Christ Jesus were baptized into his death?

- Am I not aware that just as Christ was raised from the dead by the glory of the Father, we, too, might live a new life?

PASCHA (Easter) SUNDAY

**His Eminence,† Metropolitan Judson Procyk,
from his 1995 Easter Pastoral Letter**

(Courtesy of the Byzantine Catholic World)

Early in the morning on the first day of the week, while it was still dark, Mary Magdalene came to the tomb. She saw that the stone had been moved away, so she ran off to Simon Peter and the other disciple and told them, "The Lord has been taken from the tomb. We don't know where they have put Him!"

John 20:1-2

Readings

Acts 1:1-8

John 1:1-17

Meditation

How good it is to have Mary Magdalene with us on this Easter Sunday! The story of Mary's past is well-known: the woman with a soiled identity meets the man from Galilee who makes straight the crooked lines of our lives. She is not condemned, rejected, or given a basic course in Morality 101. Jesus accepts her and loves her unconditionally. Jesus' love is nonjudgmental and a totally free gift. Jesus is not soft on sin but firm on loving in such a way that death gives way to life. That's the kind of love we need. And that's the kind of love that leads us from Good Friday to Easter Sunday. Love is stronger than death. Death does not have the last word. Hope wins out over despair. On this Easter Sunday, Mary Magdalene is with us again saying those things so human and so much like we would say. Mary, whose life has been transformed by love, comes to the tomb to minister to Jesus. However, the stone has been rolled away and Jesus is nowhere to be found.

What has happened? Simple: somebody stole Jesus' Body! In the words of Mary, "The Lord has been taken from the tomb! We don't know where they have put Him!" (*John 20:2*) Mary's statement can be a profound question for us: where has Jesus been put? Where is Jesus to be found in our world and in our lives?

Icon of the Descent into Hades (Resurrection)

We are some two thousand years removed from that Easter morning. We easily (perhaps too easily) proclaim that Jesus is risen. We can offer a wagging head at Mary's response. Why didn't she and the others know that Jesus was alive?

John offers an answer: the Spirit had not yet been given, so their understanding of Jesus was inadequate. However, we pride ourselves on having the Spirit. We claim to know and to be enlightened about the things above. Such claims of knowledge also bring claims of greater responsibility. Hence, we turn to Mary's statement: the Lord is not in the tomb. Where is Jesus to be found?

Jesus is to be found in all those multiple places and events in which life overcomes death; love transforms hatred; hope dispels fear and faith moves us to proclaim with courage that Jesus is our Lord. The risen Lord is to be found in our hospitals where countless men and women minister God's healing love. The risen Lord is to be found in our prisons where so many need spiritual liberation and guidance so life can begin anew.

The risen Lord is found in our homes through the quiet heroism and saintliness of families who share God's love with each other. The risen Lord is to be found in schools and workplaces where countless individuals do all with courage for the greater glory of God and the love of their neighbors. In all of these, and innumerable other ways, the risen Lord becomes present once again in our history and heart. Easter's basic message is one of hope. In the words of Peter: "everyone who believes in Him has forgiveness of sins through his name." (*Acts 10:43*) Paul puts it in the following way: "When Christ our life appears, then you shall appear with Him in glory." (*Colossians 3:4*) For now we are aware of the reality of death. We know that many suffer and are wounded by injustice and indifference.

We all fall short of God's glory. Yet we have been given permission to hope and believe in love. This permission comes from the One Who is not to be found among the dead. We can hope because the tomb is empty and Jesus is found among the living.

Christ is Risen!   *Indeed He is Risen!*

Patristic Reading

If there be any devout people who love God, let them enjoy this splendid and radiant Feast. If any of them be wise servants, let them blissfully enter into the joy of their Lord. If any of them have labored long in fasting let them now receive their reward. If any have toiled from the first hour, let them now receive their just wage. If any came at the third hour, let them gratefully join in the Feast. If any arrived at the sixth hour, they should not be afraid, for they will not be deprived of anything. If any of them tarried even until the ninth hour, let them approach without hesitation. If any arrived only at the eleventh hour, they should not worry on account of their tardiness. For the Master loves to grant honors and will receive the last just as the first. He gives rest to the one who came at the eleventh hour, just as He does to the one who toiled from the first hour. He shows his mercy to the last and his care for the first. To the one He gives; on the other, He showers gifts. He accepts deeds and welcomes intentions. He honors labors and praises resolutions.

And so, let all enter into the joy of their Lord, and let the first as well as the last receive the reward. Let the rich and the poor celebrate together. Let the resourceful and the slothful honor this Day. Let those who fasted and those who did not fast be glad today. The table is bountifully set; let all be satisfied. The calf is fattened; let no one go away hungry. Let everyone enjoy the cup of faith. Let everyone receive the richness of grace. Let none grieve at the poverty, for the kingdom that belongs to all people has been revealed. Let none weep for their sins, for forgiveness shines forth from the tomb. Let no one fear death, for the Savior's death has set us free.

The One Whom death imprisoned has extinguished death. The One Who descended into Hades made Hades the captive. He caused it distress when it tasted his flesh. When Isaiah foresaw this, he exclaimed: "Hades was all distressed by encountering You in the nether world." It was distressed because it was abolished. It was distressed because it was mocked. It was distressed because it was slain. It was distressed because it was overthrown. It was distressed because it was chained. It seized a body but discovered God. It seized the earthly but encountered the heavenly. It seized the visible but was overcome by the invisible. O Death, where is your sting? O Hades, where is your victory? Christ is risen, and you are abolished! Christ is risen, and the demons are cast down! Christ is risen, and the angels rejoice! Christ is risen, and life now reigns! Christ is risen, and the tomb is emptied of the dead! For in rising from the dead, Christ became the first fruits of those who have fallen asleep. To Him be glory and power forever and ever! Amen.

Resurrection Homily of John Chrysostom

THE PASCHAL SEASON

Steven Puluka

At your conception, O Lord God, an angel said to her who is full of grace: Rejoice! At your Resurrection an angel rolled away the stone from the door of your glorious tomb. The first angel spoke with signs of joy instead of sorrow, and the latter brought us the good news of a Lord who gives life instead of death. Therefore, we shout to You, O Benefactor of all, glory to You, O Lord.

Matins of Bright Monday at the Praises, Tone 2

The season of repentance and fasting before the Feast of the Resurrection is well known and observed by all Christians. We enter into the preparations for the Feast of Feasts with a humble and contrite heart and a resolve to conquer the power of food over our lives by fasting. Less well-known is the Paschal Season of equal length that follows Pascha. The Paschal Season is the forty-day period, from Pascha 'til Ascension Thursday, where fasting is abrogated and the joy of the Resurrection is to fill all of the corners of our lives. We proclaim "Christ is Risen" numerous times at every liturgical celebration as a constant reminder of the meaning of life.

The Period of the Fast is over, and the season of celebration begins. For forty days, we fasted and spiritually prepared for the act of redemption. Now the "Great Day" has arrived, and we celebrate the Feast of Feasts with jubilation for another forty days. We carry the message of joy to the entire world that Christ is Risen! But the Paschal Season is also a continuing reflection on the incomprehensible act of salvation and God's love for the world.

We should be like the disciples on the road to Emmaus. We have walked with and have been taught by the Lord Jesus on the holy road of the Great Fast. He journeyed with Cleopas and the other disciple to Emmaus, calming their fears and giving them the final teaching that explained all that they had witnessed.

Then, in a flash, at the breaking of the bread, they realized the magnitude of all that God had done for them. Suddenly, knowing the fullness of Truth, they felt compelled to share the Good News with the other disciples still in Jerusalem. So strong was their desire to share this knowledge that they left immediately, in the dark, for the Holy City. So great was their joy, so great their intention of heralding the Good News about Jesus, they could not even wait until morning!

This is precisely the spirit of the resurrectional period. And such should be the fervor that must be instilled into our hearts. This resurrectional spirit has been the impetus for the Church's growth throughout the ages. Proclaiming this news about the Risen Lord was an all-consuming passion even when it meant death to the messenger. Death has been conquered; Death reigns no more!

This faith keeps us from despair and free from the absurd. The Radiant Resurrection of Christ is the very foundation of the Church and each of its faithful. All of our hope rests on the reality of the Holy Resurrection. In the spirit of the Life-Creating Resurrection, we must exude the Good News about Jesus in all we say and do. Eternal Life, the gift of the Lord's Resurrection, is meant to be shared with all peoples. We must radiate the same God-given joy that the disciples did on the road to Emmaus on that first "Great Day".